MORPU

Michael Morpurgo

MORPURGO: WAR PLAYS

PRIVATE PEACEFUL
TORO! TORO!
THE MOZART QUESTION

Adapted by Simon Reade

OBERON BOOKS
LONDON

WWW.OBERONBOOKS.COM

This collection first published in 2012 by Oberon Books Ltd
Private Peaceful first published in 2006 by Oberon Books Ltd
521 Caledonian Road, London N7 9RH
Tel: +44 (0) 20 7607 3637 / Fax: +44 (0) 20 7607 3629
e-mail: info@oberonbooks.com / www.oberonbooks.com

A catalogue record for this book is available from the British Library.

PB ISBN: 978-1-84943-390-7
E ISBN: 978-1-84943-541-3

Cover image by Matt Humphrey from the feature film *Private
Peaceful*, a Fluidity Films production.

Printed, bound and converted
by CPI Group (UK) Ltd, Croydon, CR0 4YY.

Visit www.oberonbooks.com to read more about all our books
and to buy them. You will also find features, author interviews and
news of any author events, and you can sign up for e-newsletters
so that you're always first to hear about our new releases.

for Rose, Amy, Hazel and Otto

Contents

Introduction

Michael Morpurgo's stories move from happiness and joy to human catastrophe in an inkling. He tells his tales through the eyes of adults and the eyes of a child – often one and the same, simultaneously. His writing is intensely dramatic, his characters endure extraordinary psychological journeys, and he is unflinching in his pursuit of emotional truth. This, combined with characteristic exuberance and *joie de vivre*, is what makes his work so theatrical and why I am irresistibly drawn to dramatise it.

Private Peaceful is set before and during the First World War – known as The Great War at the beginning of the twentieth century, in the vain hope that there would be no more wars after this 'war to end all wars'. At the end of Tommo's story, as he faces the ultimate adversity, we nonetheless hold faith that humanity must one day cease to send its young to unjust slaughter.

Toro! Toro! is set in a Civil – or Uncivil – War: brother against brother, family against family, Spaniard against Spaniard. And the Spanish Civil War also lured idealists from all over the world who had never before raised arms against anyone, who were now fighting for one ideology (International Socialism) against another (Fascism).

The Mozart Question features an adult musician, a violinist, whose Jewish parents have been snagged in a Europe devastated by the Second World War and its Holocaust. Yet even in the depths of their despair they can acknowledge the redemption that can be offered by their music.

Each of these three plays for one actor playing umpteen roles is inspired, if that can be the appropriate word, by the shock of war. Wars are ostensibly fought in pursuit of ideals but are always rendered absurd by the adults who take us to war, by their bankrupt morality and cynical materialism and casual indifference. It is the clarity of vision of the children who endure these wars, are orphaned in them, slaughtered in them, survive them against the odds, who are our beacon of hope. It is in these children and their future that the ideals to which we aspire are enshrined – and should never be corrupted to fuel the indecency of war. In telling these stories in the theatre, we bear collective witness to the tenacity of the human imagination, to the passion of the human heart, to the triumph of the human spirit – to the bright spark of humanity that urges us through the dark night of the soul.

Simon Reade, 2012

PRIVATE PEACEFUL

Finding Private Peaceful

I was born in 1943, near London. I played in bomb sites, listened to the stories told around the kitchen table, stories of war that saddened all the faces around me. My Uncle Pieter lived only in the photo on the mantelpiece. He had been killed in the RAF in 1941. But for me he lived on, ever young in the photograph, as I grew up, as I grew old.

So I have been drawn instinctively, I think, in many of my stories, to the subject of war, the enduring of it, the pity of it, and above all the suffering of survivors. Some thirty years ago, after meeting an old soldier from my village who had been to the First World War in the Devon Yeomanry in the Cavalry, I wrote *War Horse*, a vision of that dreadful war seen through the eyes of a horse.

Then, almost ten years ago, on a visit to Ypres to talk about writing about war for young people at a conference, I visited the In Flanders Fields Museum.

Talking to Piet Chielens, its director, I was reminded that over 300 British soldiers had been executed during the First World War for cowardice or desertion, two of them for simply falling asleep at their posts.

I read their stories, their trials (some lasted less than twenty minutes – twenty minutes for a man's life). They knew then about shell shock – many officers were treated in psychiatric hospitals for it, Wilfred Owen and Siegfried Sassoon amongst them. They knew even as they sentenced these men (they called them 'worthless' men), that most of them were traumatized by the terrors they had endured, by the prolonged and dreadful brutality of trench warfare.

In all, over 3,000 were condemned to death, and 300 of them were chosen to be shot. I visited the execution sites, the cells in Poperinghe, I read the telegram sent home to a mother informing her that her son had been shot at dawn for cowardice. I knew recent governments had considered and rejected the granting of pardons for these men, had refused to acknowledge the appalling injustice visited upon them.

Standing in a war cemetery in the rain five miles outside Ypres, I came upon the gravestone of Private Peaceful. I had found my name, my Unknown Soldier. I had found my story, a story I knew I had to tell and that should be told.

The question then was how it should be told. I decided to put myself at the centre of the story, to become the condemned man waiting only for dawn and death. A glance at my watch, recently returned from the menders who had declared it was made in 1915, gave me the idea that the chapter breaks should happen only when the soldier glances down at his watch which he dreads to do, and tries not to do.

My soldier would reflect on his life, live it again through the night so that the night would be long, as long as his life. He does not want to sleep his last night away, nor waste it in dreams. Above all he wants to feel alive.

Each chapter begins in the barn in Belgium, but his thoughts soon take him back to Devon, to the fields and streams and lanes of Iddesleigh, his home and his village.

Memories of his childhood come back to him, of family. Of the first day at school, of the first stirrings of love, a father's death, a night's poaching; then of the first news of approaching war and the recruiting sergeant in the town square at Hatherleigh. So to the trenches and to the events that have led him to the last night of his life.

And all the while the watch he does not want to look at is ticking his life away.

Michael Morpurgo

In the First World War, between 1914 and 1918, over 290 soldiers of the British and Commonwealth armies were executed by firing squad, some for desertion, some for cowardice, two for simply sleeping at their posts.

Many of these men were traumatized by shell shock. Courts martial were brief, the accused often unrepresented.

The injustice they suffered at the start of the twentieth century was only officially recognised by the British Government at the beginning of the twenty-first century and some ninety years later the men were granted posthumous pardons.

Private Peaceful was first performed on 7 April 2004 at Bristol Old Vic's Studio theatre, with the following company:

TOMMO, Paul Chequer

Director, Simon Reade
Designer, Bill Talbot
Lighting Designer, Tim Streader
Sound Designer, Jason Barnes
Stage Manager, Juliette Taylor
Production Manager, Jo Cuthbert
Studio Technician, Olly Hellis
Casting Advisor, Amy Ball
Dialect, Charmian Hoare

The production has subsequently toured throughout the UK with Scamp Theatre and played in Ireland, Off-Broadway, Hong Kong and Wellington, New Zealand, with Tommo played by Alexander Campbell, Finn Hanlon, Mark Quartley and Leon Williams.

Thanks to Michael and Clare Morpurgo, Alison Reid, Rose and Amy Reade, David Farr and Mark Leipacher.

Characters

TOMMO

Note

The actor playing Tommo delivers all the lines in the play. Other characters' speech is indicated thus:

(CHARACTER NAME.)

The style of the production is to tell the story as simply as possible, with the set and props pared down to the military clothes the performer stands up in, and the bed Tommo lies in – which is turned on its side for the trench, for example. The rest of Tommo's world is created by engaging the audience's imagination.

Private Peaceful

Ypres. 1916. No-man's-land.
24ᵗʰ June. A barn, a prison. A bed. A bully tin of stew, potatoes.
A pair of boots.

1

(*Private Peaceful – TOMMO, nearly 18 – looks at his watch.*)

BARN

Five past ten.

I have the whole night ahead of me. I shan't sleep. I won't dream it away.

I want to remember everything, just as it was, just as it happened. I've had nearly eighteen years of yesterdays and tomorrows, and tonight I must remember as many of them as I can.

Tonight, more than any other night of my life, I want to feel alive!

ON THE WAY TO SCHOOL

Charlie's leading me by the hand because he knows I don't want to go (to school). I've never worn a collar before and it's choking me. My boots are strange and heavy on my feet. My heart's heavy too. I'm dreading it.

Big Joe doesn't have to go and I don't think that's fair at all. He's much older than me, even a bit older than Charlie. But Big Joe stays at home with Mother, and sits up in his tree singing 'Oranges and Lemons'. He's always laughing. I wish I could be happy like him. I wish I could be at home like him. I don't want to go with Charlie. I DON'T WANT TO GO TO SCHOOL.

Charlie sees my eyes full of tears and knows how it is. He's three years older than me, so he's done everything, knows everything.

(CHARLIE.) Do you want a piggyback, Tommo?

I hop up and cling on tight round Charlie's neck, trying not to whimper.

(CHARLIE.) First day's the worst, Tommo. It's not so bad. Honest.

Whenever Charlie says 'honest', I know it's not true.

(*Sound: bell.*)

OUTSIDE SCHOOL

We line up in two silent rows, about twenty children in each. I recognize some of them from Sunday school. Charlie's no longer beside me. He's in the other line, and he's winking at me. I blink back. I can't wink with one eye. Charlie laughs.

(MR MUNNINGS.) Fall into line!

Mr Munnings: he of the raging temper Charlie's told me so much about. Mr Munnings is pointing right at me and all the other children have turned to look.

(MR MUNNINGS.) Ah! A new boy. A new boy to add to my trials and tribulations. Name, boy?

(TOMMO.) Tommo, sir. Thomas Peaceful.

(MR MUNNINGS.) First a Charlie Peaceful, and now a Thomas Peaceful. Was not one Peaceful enough? Understand this, Thomas Peaceful, that here I am your lord and master. You do what I say when I say it. You do not cheat, you do not lie, you do not blaspheme. These are my commandments. Do I make myself clear?

(TOMMO.) Yes, sir.

Charlie and the big'uns follow Mr Munnings into one classroom. And then I'm taken with the tiddlers into Miss McAllister's.

CLASSROOM

(MISS MCALLISTER.) Thomas, you will be sitting here –

– Miss McAllister is very proper –

(MISS MCALLISTER.) – sitting there, next to Molly. And your bootlaces are undone. Tie them up before you trip.

(TOMMO.) I can't, miss.

(MISS MCALLISTER.) 'Can't' is not a word we use in my class, Thomas Peaceful. We shall just have to teach you how to tie your bootlaces. That's what we're all here for, Thomas: to learn. You show him, Molly. Molly's the oldest girl in my class, Thomas. She'll help you.

Molly doesn't look up at me while she's tying them – but I wish she would. She has chestnut-brown hair the same colour as Father's old horse – and shining – and I want to reach out and touch it. Then at last she looks up at me. I have a friend.

(*Sound: schoolyard; kids playing.*)

SCHOOLYARD

In playtime, in the schoolyard, I want to go over and talk to Molly, but I can't because she's surrounded by a gaggle of giggling girls. They keep looking over their shoulders and laughing at me. I look for Charlie, but he's playing conkers with the big'uns. So I decide to undo my bootlaces and try doing them up again like Molly. I try again and again. It's untidy, it's loose – but I can do it! From across the schoolyard Molly sees, and smiles.

At home I never wear boots, except for church. Father always wore his great hobnail boots, the boots he died in.

IN THE WOODS

In the woods, Father was chopping away at a tree nearby, grunting and groaning at every stroke. At first I think he's just groaning a bit louder. But then the sound seems to be coming from somewhere high up in the branches.

I look up: the great tree is swaying and creaking when all the other trees are standing still, silent. I stand and stare.

(*Sound: tree falling like a roar of thunder.*)

(FATHER.) Run, Tommo! Run!

(*Silence. The tree has fallen.*)

When I came to, I see him at once, see the soles of his boots with their worn nails. One arm is outstretched towards me, his finger points at me. His eyes are open, but I know they're not seeing me. He's not breathing. When I shout at him, when I shake him, he doesn't wake up.

(*Sound: solemn harmonium hymn.*)

CHURCH

In the church we're sat side by side at the front, Mother, Big Joe, Charlie and me. We've never in our lives sat in the front row before. It's where the Colonel always sits. The coffin rests on trestles, Father inside in his Sunday suit. A swallow swoops over our heads all through the prayers and the hymns, flitting from window to window, to belfry, to altar, looking for a way out. And I know for certain it is Father trying to escape. I know because he told us more than once that in his next life he'd like to be a bird, so he could fly free wherever he wanted.

The Colonel gets up into the pulpit:

(COLONEL. *Thumb tucked behind jacket lapel.*) James Peaceful was a good man, one of the best workers I have known, the salt of the earth, always cheerful as he went about his work. The Peaceful family has been employed by my family for five generations. In all his thirty years as a forester on my estate James Peaceful was a credit to his family and village.

While the Colonel's droning on I'm thinking of all the rude things Father used to say about him –

(FATHER.) – silly old fart, mad old duffer –

– and how Mother always said that –

(MOTHER.) – he might well be a 'silly old fart', but it's the Colonel who pays the wages and owns the roof over our heads, so you all show him respect.

GRAVEYARD

The earth thumps down on the coffin (behind us) as we leave the graveside. He was trying to save me. If only I had run, he wouldn't now be lying dead.

All I've ever thought is that I killed my own father.

2

(*TOMMO looks at his watch.*)

BARN

Twenty to eleven.

(*He spoons his food unenthusiastically.*)

I don't want to eat. Stew, potatoes. I usually like stew, but I've no appetite. Not now.

Big Joe ate more than all the rest of us put together – potato pie, cheese and pickle, stew and dumplings, bread and butter pudding – whatever Mother cooked, he'd stuff it in and scoff it down. Anything Charlie and I didn't like we'd shuffle onto his plate when Mother wasn't looking.

Mother told us when we were older that Big Joe nearly died just after he was born. 'Meningitis', the doctor told her at the hospital, 'brain damage'.

She was told 'he wouldn't live or even if he did, he'd be of no use to anyone.'

It was Big Joe who got me into my first fight.

(*Sound: schoolyard; kids playing.*)

SCHOOLYARD

It was playtime. Big Joe had come up to school to see Charlie and me. He stood and watched us from outside the gate, bright-eyed with excitement. I ran over to him. He opened his cupped hands just enough for me to see a slow-worm curled inside.

(TOMMO.) That's lovely, Joe.

Then Big Joe wandered off, walking down the lane, humming:

(BIG JOE. *Humming.*) Oranges and Lemons (*Etc.*)

Someone taps me hard on my shoulder.

(JIMMY PARSONS. *Sneering.*) Who's got a loony for a brother?

(TOMMO.) What did you say, Jimmy Parsons?

(JIMMY PARSONS. *Chanting.*) Your-brother's-a-loony, your-brother's-a-loony.

So I go for him, fists flailing, screaming – but I don't land a single punch. Then Jimmy Parsons hits me full in the face and sends me sprawling. He puts the boot in, kicking and kicking –

– then, suddenly, he stops.

I look up. Charlie's grabbing him round the neck and pulling him to the ground. They're rolling over and over, punching each other and blaspheming. The whole school has gathered round to watch now, shouting and egging them on. 'Go on, Charlie!'

That's when Mr Munnings comes running out, roaring.

(MR MUNNINGS.) What the blazes!

He pulls them apart and drags them off inside the school.

Luckily for me, Mr Munnings never even notices me, bleeding.

They both get the cane, six strokes each.

Molly comes over, takes me by the hand and leads me towards the pump. She soaks her handkerchief under it and dabs my nose and my hands and my knee – the blood is everywhere. The water is cold and soothing, and her hands are soft.

(MOLLY.) I like Big Joe. He's kind. I like people who are kind.

Molly likes Big Joe! It was then that I knew I would love her till the day I die.

Then Charlie comes out into the schoolyard hitching up his trousers and grinning in the sunshine.

(CHARLIE.) Jimmy won't do it again, Tommo. I hit him where it hurts. In the goolies.

We all laughed at that.

(CHARLIE.) Are you all right, Tommo?

(TOMMO.) My nose hurts a bit, Charlie.

(CHARLIE.) Well, so does my bum.

COUNTRYSIDE

Back home we were getting very hungry, without Father. We tried to make ends meet, but all we ever seemed to have for supper were potatoes.

So Charlie had the idea to go poaching. By now, we were best friends with Molly, so she came too. At dusk, or dawn, we'd go off across the Colonel's land, into his forests, fishing in his river. Molly and I would be on look-out while Charlie did the trapping or netting.

We did well. We caught loads of rabbits, a few trout and, once, a fourteen-pound salmon. So now we had something to eat with our potatoes.

MEADOWS

Both of them being older than me – Molly by two years, Charlie by three – they always ran faster than I did, racing ahead of me, leaping the high meadow grass, Molly's plaits whirling about her head, their laughter mingling. When they got too far ahead I sometimes felt they wanted to be without me. But I'd whine and they'd soon wait for me to catch up. Best of all Molly would (sometimes) come running back and take my hand.

BROOK

We'd hare down the hill to the brook, pull off our heavy boots and release our aching feet. We'd sit there on the bank wiggling our toes in the cool water. Then we'd follow the brook home, feet squelching in the mud, our toes oozing with it. I used to love mud, the smell of it, the feel of it, the larking about in it.

RIVERSIDE / POOL

Sometimes we'd go swimming in the river's pool, hung all around by willows, where the water was dark and deep and mysterious, and where no one ever came.

One time, Molly dared Charlie to take off all his clothes – and to my amazement, he did! Then she did!! – and they both ran shrieking and bare-bottomed into the water. When they called me in after them, I wouldn't do it, not in front of Molly. So I sat and sulked on the bank and watched them splashing and giggling, wishing I was with them. Eventually, they persuaded me. Molly stood waist-deep in the river and put her hands over her eyes.

(MOLLY.) Come on, Tommo! I won't watch. Promise.

I stripped off and made a dash for the river, covering myself as I went just in case Molly was peeping through her fingers.

Afterwards, Molly got dressed behind a bush and told us 'not to watch'. But we did. That was the first time I ever saw a girl with no clothes on. She was very thin and white, and she wrung her plaits out like a wet cloth.

Molly told us she wanted to die right there and then, which I thought a little strange, but she explained:

(MOLLY.) I never want tomorrow to come because no tomorrow will ever be as good as today.

She collected a handful of small pebbles from the shallows of the river.

(MOLLY.) I'm going to tell the future. I've seen the gypsies do it.

> (*She shakes the pebbles around in her cupped hands, closes her eyes and then scatters them out on to the muddy shore.*)

(MOLLY.) The stones say we'll always be together, the three of us, for ever and ever. They say that as long as we all stick together we'll all be lucky and happy. And the stones never lie. So you're stuck with me.

> (*Sound: summer buzz; animals and birds.*)

BROOK / MEADOW

Another time, Molly and Charlie and I were fishing down in the brook. It was late on a summer evening and we were just about to set off home when we heard the distant sound of an engine.

> (*Sound: intermittent droning, like a thousand stuttering bees.*)

At first we thought it was the Colonel's car – his Rolls-Royce was the only car for miles around – but it wasn't coming from the road at all; it was coming from somewhere high above us.

An aeroplane!

It circled above us like some ungainly yellow bird. We could see the goggled pilot looking down at us out of the cockpit. We waved up at him and he waved back. Then he seemed to be flying towards us, lower, lower.

It bounced, then bumped, then came to a stop just in front of us. The pilot beckoned us over.

(PILOT. *Shouting over the roar of the engine.*) Better not switch off! Might never get the damn thing started again. Listen, the truth is, I reckon I'm a bit lost. That church up there on the hill, is that Lapford church?

(CHARLIE. *Shouting back.*) No, that's Iddesleigh. St James's.

(PILOT. *Shouting.*) Iddesleigh? You sure?

(CHARLIE. *Shouting.*) Yes!

(PILOT. *Shouting.*) Whoops! Then I really was lost. Jolly good thing I stopped, wasn't it? Thanks for your help. Better be off. Here. Do you like humbugs?

And he handed us a bag of sweets.

(PILOT. *Shouting.*) Cheerio then. Stand well back. Here we go.

(*Sound: the plane splutters off.*)

He went bouncing along towards the hedge – and lifted off just in time, his wheels clipping the top, before he was up, up, and away. He did one steep turn, then flew straight at us. We threw ourselves face down in the long grass, feeling the blast of the wind as he flew over us. By the time we rolled over he was climbing up over the trees, over St James's church tower and away into the distance. And then he was gone.

(*Sound: just the buzzing summer silence again. A skylark sings.*)

For some time afterwards we lay there in the long grass watching a single skylark rising above us as we sucked on our humbugs.

(TOMMO.) Was that real, Charlie? Did it really happen?

(CHARLIE.) We've got our humbugs, Tommo, so it must have been real, mustn't it?

3

BARN

Ten to midnight.

I'm not sure I ever really believed in God, even in Sunday school. In church I'd gaze up at Jesus hanging on the cross in the stained-glass window, and feel sorry for him because I could see how cruel it was and how much it must be hurting him. I knew he was a good and kind man. But what I never really understood was why God, who was supposed to be his father, and almighty and powerful, would let them do that to him, would let him suffer so much. I believed then, as I believe now, that crossed fingers and Molly's stones are every bit as reliable or unreliable as praying to God. But if there's no God, does that mean there's no heaven? Tonight I want to believe there's a heaven; that there is a new life after death, like Father said, that death is not a full stop.

HOME

After my twelfth birthday, Charlie and Molly left school. I was alone, a big'un in Mr Munnings' class. I hated him now more than I feared him. Charlie and Molly found work up in the Big House: Molly as an under-parlour maid, and Charlie in the Colonel's hunt kennels.

Charlie would come home late in the cold evenings, hang up his coat on Father's peg and put his boots outside in the porch where Father's boots had always been and warm his feet in the bottom oven, just as Father had done. That was the first time in my life I was ever really jealous of Charlie. I wanted to warm my feet in the oven, to come home from proper work, to earn money like Charlie did. Most of all though I wanted Charlie and Molly and me to be together again, for everything to be just as it had been. (But nothing stays the same.)

When I did see Molly, and it was only on Sundays now, she was as kind to me as she'd always been, but too kind almost, more like a mother to me than a friend. Her hair was cut shorter now, the plaits were gone, and that changed the whole look of her. Molly wasn't a girl any more.

Then Charlie had a serious run-in with the Colonel and left his job up at the Big House and found work at Farmer Cox's on the other side of the village, so I saw even less of him than before. But we didn't see Molly at all any more. She'd suddenly stopped coming round – so Charlie sent me to her cottage with a letter.

OUTSIDE MOLLY'S COTTAGE

Molly's mother met me at the door:

(MOLLY'S MOTHER. *Her face like thunder.*) Go away. Just go away. We don't want you Peacefuls here. We don't want you bothering our Molly. And she doesn't want to see you. Go on!

I was walking away, Charlie's letter in my pocket, when I happened to glance back: Molly was waving at me frantically through her window, mouthing something I couldn't understand, pointing down the hill towards the brook.

BROOK

I ran down and waited. Molly soon arrived, hot and bothered:

(MOLLY.) The Colonel came to our cottage and told mother and father that he had dismissed Charlie because he had been seeing more of me than was good for me. They won't let me see Charlie any more. They won't let me see any of you. I'm so miserable without you, Tommo. I hate it up at the Big House, and I hate it at home too.

I leant over and kissed her on the cheek. She threw her arms around me, sobbing as if her heart would break.

(MOLLY.) I want to see Charlie. I miss him so much.

It was only then that I remembered to give her the letter. She tore it open and read it at once.

(MOLLY.) Tell him yes. Yes, I will.

That was the first of dozens of letters I delivered from Charlie to Molly and from Molly to Charlie over the weeks and months that followed. I was their go-between postman. Molly and I would meet most evenings and exchange letters in the same place, down by the brook. We'd sit and talk for a few precious minutes, often with the rain dripping through the trees. Once the wind roared so violently that I feared the trees might come down on us, so we ran out across the meadow and burrowed our way under a haystack and sat there shivering like a couple of frightened rabbits. It was in the shelter of this haystack that I first heard about the war.

It was Molly's job every morning to iron the Colonel's newspaper before she took it to him in his study – he insisted his *Times* should be crisp and dry, so that the ink would not come off on his fingers while he was reading it. I didn't really know about the war, but I learned that some archduke – whatever that was – had been shot in a place called Sarajevo – wherever that was – and Germany and France – I knew where they were – were very angry with each other about it. They were gathering their armies to fight each other and, if they did, then Great Britain would soon be in it too because we'd have to fight on the French side against the Germans.

In the meantime there were bigger bombshells closer to home.

HAY FIELD / HOME

Charlie and I had been haymaking with Farmer Cox – I was working with Charlie now; I'd finally left school and Mr Munnings far behind me. I'd thought about working for the Colonel: five generations of Peacefuls, six including Charlie, had done so before me; and it was tempting to work with

Molly. But I knew I wanted to work alongside Charlie more than anything else in the world – So, we were haymaking with Farmer Cox, buzzards wheeling above us all day long, swallows skimming the mown grass, as if Father was there watching over us. When we arrived home later than usual, dusty and hungry, Mother was sitting bolt upright in her chair doing her sewing and opposite her: Molly – a leather suitcase under the window sill.

(TOMMO.) What is it? What's up?

Molly didn't answer me. Mother spoke for her:

(MOTHER.) They've thrown her out. The Colonel, her mother and father have thrown her out, and it's your fault, Charlie.

Charlie looked confused:

(CHARLIE.) What's happened? What's going on?

Molly shook her head. Charlie looked at Mother. Mother looked at Charlie:

(MOTHER.) What's going on, Charlie, is that she's going to have your baby, that's what.

BEDROOM

That night I lay there in our room beside Charlie, not speaking. I was so filled with anger towards him that I never wanted to speak to him, nor Molly, ever again. Then Charlie spoke:

(CHARLIE.) It wasn't just letters, Tommo, you see... We didn't want to hide it from you, Tommo, honest. But we didn't want to hurt you either. Because you love her, don't you? Well, so do I, Tommo. I love her. Friends?

(*Pause.*)

(TOMMO.) Friends.

CHURCH

They were married up in the church a short time later, a very empty church. There was no one there except the vicar and the five of us, and the vicar's wife sitting at the back. Everyone knew about the baby by now, so the vicar only agreed to marry them on certain conditions: 'that no bells are rung, no hymns sung'. He rushed through the marriage service as if he wanted to be somewhere else. There was no wedding feast afterwards, only a cup of tea and a slice of fruit cake when we got home.

BIG JOE'S ROOM

I moved into Big Joe's room and slept with him in his bed, which wasn't easy because Big Joe was big, and the bed very narrow. He talked loudly to himself in his dreams, and tossed and turned all night long. But, as I lay awake, what troubled me more was that in the next room slept the two people I loved most in all the world who, in finding each other, had deserted me.

At home, I tried never to be alone with Molly – I didn't know what to say to her any more. I tried to avoid Charlie, too. On the farm, I took every opportunity that came my way to work on my own. Farmer Cox was always sending me off on some errand or other and I always took my time about it.

MARKET

It was while I was making a delivery to Hatherleigh market (one morning) that I came face to face with the war for the first time.

(*Sound: market noise; drums pounding, bugles blaring.*)

Behind the band there must have been a dozen soldiers, splendid in their scarlet uniforms. They marched past me, arms swinging in perfect time, polished buttons, boots shining, the sun glinting on their bayonets. Children were stomping alongside them, some in paper hats, some with wooden sticks over their shoulders. And there were women throwing flowers, roses mostly, their thorns hooking to the soldiers' tunics. Everyone followed.

(*Sound: band plays 'God Save the King'.*)

The Union Jack fluttering behind him, the first sergeant major I'd ever set eyes on got up on to the steps in the middle of the town square.

(SERGEANT MAJOR. *Commanding.*) Ladies and gentlemen, boys and girls! I shan't beat about the bush. I shan't tell you it's all tickety-boo out there in France – there's been too much of that nonsense already in my view. I've been there. I've seen it for myself. So I'll tell you straight. It's no picnic. It's an 'ard slog. But there's only one question to ask yourself about this war. Who would you rather see marching through your streets? Us lot, or the Hun? Because, mark my words, ladies and gentlemen, if we don't stop them out there in France, the Germans will be here, right here on your doorstep. They'll come marching through burning your houses, violating your women, killing your children. They've beaten brave little Belgium, swallowed her up in one gulp. And now they've taken a fair slice of France too. Unless we beat them at their own game, they'll gobble us up as well. Well? Do you want the Hun here? Do you?

'No!' came the shout, and I was shouting along with them.

(SERGEANT MAJOR.) Shall we beat the living daylights out of them then?

'Yes!' we roared.

(SERGEANT MAJOR.) Good. Then we shall need you. (*Pointing, like Kitchener, into the crowd.*) Your King needs you. Your country needs you. And all the brave lads out in France need you too. (*His face breaks into a smile.*) And remember one thing, lads – and I can vouch for this – all the ladies love a soldier.

The girls all laughed and giggled. The young men blushed.

(SERGEANT MAJOR.) So, who'll be the first brave lad to come and take the King's shilling? Who'll lead the way? I'm looking for boys with hearts of oak, lads who love their King and country, men what hates the lousy Hun.

Then the first one stepped forward. I recognised him at once: it was big Jimmy Parsons, the boy Charlie had hit in the goolies. Egged on by the cheering crowd, others soon followed.

Suddenly someone prods me hard in the small of my back – a toothless old lady is pointing at me with her crooked finger.

(TOOTHLESS OLD LADY. *Croaking.*) Go on, son, you go and fight. It's every man's duty to fight when his country calls, that's what I say. Go on. Y'ain't a coward, are you?

I didn't run, not at first. I sidled away from her slowly, backing out of the crowd hoping no one would notice me.

(TOOTHLESS OLD LADY.) Chicken! Chicken!

Then I ran helter-skelter from the crowded square, down the deserted High Street.

(TOOTHLESS OLD LADY.) Chicken!

Filled with shame, I keep on going, the Toothless Old Lady's words ringing in my ears, thinking about what the Sergeant Major has said, about how fine and manly the men looked, how Molly would admire me in my scarlet uniform, maybe even love me if I joined up. I ran all the way home.

KITCHEN

We'd barely sat down for supper before I began:

(TOMMO.) Farmer Cox sent me to market this morning. The army was there, recruiting. Jimmy Parsons joined up. Lots of others too.

Then Mother interrupted me:

(MOTHER.) Don't worry about it, Tommo, they can't make you go. You're too young anyway.

(TOMMO.) I'm nearly sixteen.

(CHARLIE.) You've got to be nineteen to serve overseas, Tommo, they don't want boys.

(I guessed Charlie was right.) Then Molly joined in, her hand resting on her pregnant belly:

(MOLLY.) They shouldn't take the men either. What are the women supposed to do, fend for themselves? What about the mothers? You wouldn't go Charlie, would you?

(CHARLIE.) I'll be honest, Moll. It's been bothering me a lot just lately. I don't want to go. I'd shoot a rat because it might bite me. I'd shoot a rabbit because I can eat it. Why would I ever want to shoot a German? Never even met a German. But I've seen the lists in the papers – y'know, all the killed and the wounded. Pages of them. Poor beggars. It hardly seems right, does it: me being here, enjoying life, while they're over there. (It's not all bad, Moll.) I saw Benny Copplestone yesterday, sporting his uniform up at the pub. He's back on leave. He says we've got the Germans on the run now. One big push, he reckons, and we'll have 'em running back to Berlin with their tails between their legs, and then all our boys can come home. With a bit of luck I'll be back to wet the baby's head. And Tommo will look after you. He'll be the man about the place, won't you, Tommo?

(TOMMO.) I'm not staying, Charlie. I'm coming with you.

I loved what I knew: and what I knew was my family, and Molly, and the countryside I'd grown up in. I would do all I could to protect the people I loved. And I would do it with Charlie.

(Optional Interval.)

4

BARN

A quarter past two.

I'm not sleepy.

I should be able to fight off sleep by now. I've done it often enough on look-out in the trenches. I used to long for that moment when you surrender to sleep, when you drift away into the warmth of nothingness. After this night is over, I can drift away, I can sleep for ever.

(Sound: steam train.)

TRAIN

On the train to Exeter, Charlie gave me my instructions:

(CHARLIE.) You'll have to behave like a nineteen year old from now on, Tommo. You follow my lead.

REGIMENTAL DEPOT

When the time came, in front of the Recruiting Officer at the regimental depot, I stood as tall as I could and let Charlie speak for us both.

(CHARLIE.) I'm Charlie Peaceful, and he's Thomas Peaceful. We're twins and we're volunteering.

(RECRUITING OFFICER.) Date of birth?

(CHARLIE.) 5th of October, '95.

(RECRUITING OFFICER.) Both of you?

(CHARLIE.) Course, only I'm older than him by one hour.

And that was that. Easy. We were in.

TRAINING GROUND

(SERGEANT HANLEY.) Stand still! Stomach in, chest out! Look to your front, Peaceful, you horrible little man! Down in that mud, Peaceful, where you belong, you nasty little worm!

Sergeant Horrible Hanley. Our chief tormentor at training camp on Salisbury Plain. He would do his utmost to make all our lives a misery. And one life in particular: Charlie's.

(SERGEANT HANLEY.) Are you the best they can send us these days, Peaceful? Vermin, that's what you are. Lousy vermin, and I've got to make a soldier out of you. What's with this cap badge, Peaceful? It's crooked. You are a blot on creation, Peaceful. What are you?

(CHARLIE. *Clear, firm, utterly without fear.*) Happy to be here, Sergeant.

The boots they gave us were far too big – they hadn't got any smaller sizes. So we clomped about like clowns – clowns in tin hats and khaki.

There were dozens of others under-age in the regiment – they needed all the young men they could get. Sometimes the older lads teased me about being so young, but Charlie would give them a little look and they'd soon stop. Then Sergeant Hanley began picking on me.

We'd been drilling one morning, and were stood to attention, when Hanley grabbed my rifle:

(SERGEANT HANLEY. *Looking down the barrel.*) Dirty.

We all knew the punishment: five times at the double around the parade ground, holding your rifle above your head. After only two circuits I just couldn't keep my rifle up.

(SERGEANT HANLEY. *Bellowing.*) Every time you let that rifle fall, Peaceful, you begin the punishment again! Five more, Peaceful.

My head is swimming. My back's on fire. I'm staggering. I hear a shout:

Charlie has broken ranks and he runs at Hanley, screaming, telling him exactly what he thinks of him.

For that, Charlie was tied to a gun wheel. 'Field Punishment Number One', the Brigadier called it:

(BRIGADIER.) Private Peaceful has got off lightly. Insubordination in a time of war could be seen as mutiny, and mutiny is punishable by death, by firing squad.

As we march past him, Charlie smiles at me. I try to smile back, but no smile came. To me, Charlie looks like Jesus hanging on the cross at St James's church back home in Iddesleigh.

5

BARN

A minute past three.

I keep checking the time. Each time I do it, I put the watch to my ear and listen for the tick. It's still there, softly slicing away the seconds, then the minutes, then the hours. Charlie told me this watch would never stop, never let me down, unless I forgot to wind it. The best watch in the world, he said, a wonderful watch. But if it was such a wonderful watch it would do more than simply keep time – any old watch can do that. A truly wonderful watch would make time. Then, if it stopped, time itself would have to stand still, then this night would never have to end and morning would never come.

Charlie always said we were living on borrowed time out here.

(*Sings.*) Oranges and Lemons, say the bells of St Clement's,

You owe me five farthings, say the bells of St Martin's.
When will you pay me? say the bells of Old Bailey.
When I grow rich, say the bells of Shoreditch.
When will that be? say the bells of Stepney.
I'm sure I don't know, says the great bell of Bow.
Here comes a candle to light you to bed,
And here comes a chopper to chop off your head.
Chip, Chop, Chip, Chop, the last – man's –

They tell us we're going over to France, and we're all relieved. We're leaving Sergeant Hanley far behind us.

(*Sound: ship's horn.*)

QUAYSIDE

When our ship docks in Boulogne, every voice I hear from the quayside below us…is English, every uniform and every helmet like our own. Then, as we come down the gangplank into the fresh morning air, we see them close to: the walking wounded shuffling along the quayside towards us, some with their eyes bandaged, holding on to the shoulder of the one in front. Others lie on stretchers. One of them, puffing on a cigarette looks at me out of sunken yellow eyes:

(SOLDIER.) G'luck lads. Give 'em what for.

MARCHING TO THE FRONT

We don't stay long in France but march into Belgium.

(*Sound: two aeroplanes buzzing overhead.*)

Two aeroplanes are chasing each other in the distance. They are too far away for us to see which of them is ours. We make up our minds it's the smaller one and cheer for him madly, and I'm wondering if the pilot from the yellow plane might be up there. I can almost taste the humbugs he gave us as I watch them. I lose them in the sun – and then the smaller one spirals earthwards and our cheering instantly stops.

(Sound: estaminet hubbub.)

ESTAMINET

After arriving at rest camp, they let us out for an evening
to go into the nearest village, to an estaminet, a sort of pub,
where there's the best beer and best egg and chips in the entire
world. We stuff ourselves.

There's a girl there who smiles at me when she clears the
plates away. She's the daughter of the owner. He is very
smartly dressed and very round and very merry, like a Father
Christmas but without the beard. It's difficult to believe
she's his daughter – she's the opposite in every way: elf-like,
delicate. Charlie and me drink ourselves silly – I'm properly
drunk for the first time in my life and feel very proud of
myself. We stagger back to camp and flop off to sleep.

FRONT LINE

The next day we march towards the line – it seems as if the
road is taking us down into the earth itself, until it is a road no
more but a tunnel without a roof, a communications trench.
We have to be silent now. Not a whisper, not a word. If the
German machine-gunners spot us, we're done for. A line of
soldiers passes us coming the other way, dark-eyed men. No
need for questions. No need for answers…

We find our dug-out at last. *(He turns the bed on its side to make
the dug-out and trench.)* It has been a long, cold march. All
I want is a mug of hot sweet tea and a lie down – but with
Charlie, I'm posted on sentry duty.

TRENCH

For the first time I look out through the wire into no-man's-
land and towards the enemy trenches. Less than two hundred
yards from our front line, they tell us. There's no smoking in
the trenches at night – not unless we want our heads shot off

by snipers spotting the red glow of the cigarette tip. The night is still now.

(CHARLIE. *Whispering.*) It's a fine night for poaching, Tommo.

(*Sound: artillery.*)

Suddenly, our artillery lobs a shell over into their trenches, and they do the same back. This terrifies me. Then it happens again and in time I get used to it.

Our trench and our dug-outs have been left a right mess by the previous soldiers and we clear it all up, because of the rats. Rats. I'm the first one to find them. I am detailed to shore up a dilapidated trench wall. I plunge my shovel in and open up an entire nest of them. They come pouring out, skittering away over my boots. For a moment I'm horrified – but then I set about stamping them to death in the mud. I don't kill a single one.

Our other daily curse is lice. Each of us has to burn off his own with a lighted cigarette end. They nestle in wherever they can: the folds of your skin, the creases of your clothes. We long for a bath to drown the lot of them.

(*Sound: rain.*)

Our greatest scourge is neither rats nor lice but the unending rain. It runs like a stream along the bottom of our trench, turning it into a mud-filled ditch, a stinking gooey mud that seems to want to hold you and then suck you down and drown you.

It's Charlie who keeps us all together. He's like a big brother to everyone. Being his real brother, I could feel I live in his shadow but I don't, I live in his glow.

Word has come down from headquarters that we must send out patrols to find out what regiments have come into the line opposite us. Why we have to do this we do not know – there are spotter planes doing it almost every day. My turn soon comes up. Charlie's too. Captain Wilkie's heading the patrol and he tells us –

(CAPTAIN WILKIE.) 'We have to bring back a prisoner for questioning.'

They give us a double rum ration, and I'm warmed instantly to the roots of my hair, to my very toenails.

On the signal, we climb up over the top and crawl on our bellies through the wire.

NO-MAN'S-LAND

We snake our way forward. It takes an eternity to cross no-man's-land. I'm beginning to wonder if we'll ever find their trenches at all. We slither into a shell hole and lie doggo there for a while. We can hear Fritz talking now, and laughing – and playing music.

(*Sound: a distant gramophone plays.*)

We're close now, very close. I'm not scared – I'm excited. I'm out poaching with Charlie. I'm tensed for danger.

Then we see the wire up ahead. We wriggle through a gap and drop down into their trench.

GERMAN TRENCH

It looks deserted, but we can still hear the voices and the music. I notice their trench is much deeper than ours, wider too and more solidly constructed. I grip my rifle tight and follow Charlie along the trench, bent double like everyone else.

(TOMMO.) We're making too much noise. I can't understand why no one has heard us. Where are their sentries, for God's sake?

At that moment, a German soldier comes out of a dug-out. For a split second the Hun does nothing and neither do we. We just stand and look at one another. Then he lets out a shriek, and blunders back into the dug-out. I don't know who threw the grenade in after him, (*Sound: blast.*) but there is a blast that throws me back against the trench wall. There is screaming and firing from inside the dug-out. Then silence. The music has stopped. We peer in through the smoke. Several German soldiers are lying sprawled out, all dead – except one. He stands there naked, blood-spattered, shaking. I'm shaking. He has his hands in the air and is whimpering. Captain Wilkie throws a coat over him and bundles him out. We scrabble our way up over the top of the German trench, through the wire – and run.

NO-MAN'S-LAND

For a while I think we have got away with it – but then a flare goes up and we are caught suddenly in broad daylight. I hurl myself to the ground.

(*Sound: machine-gun rattle, rifles popping.*)

There is nowhere to hide, so we pretend to be dead. Eyes closed, I'm thinking of Molly. If I'm going to die I want my last thought to be of her. But instead I'm saying sorry to Father for what I did, that I didn't mean to kill him.

We wait till the light dies and the night is suddenly black again. Captain Wilkie gets us to our feet and we go on, running, stumbling. Then the shelling starts. We dive into a crater.

(*Sound: shelling.*)

It seems as if we have woken up the entire German army. I cower with the German and Charlie, the three of us clinging together.

(GERMAN SOLDIER.) Lieber Gott! Lieber Gott!

'Gott.' They call God by the same name. He's praying.

Then we see the Captain lying higher up the slope; Charlie goes up and turns him over:

(CAPTAIN WILKIE.) I won't make it. I'm leaving it to you to get them all back, Peaceful, and the prisoner. Go on now.

(CHARLIE.) No, sir. If one goes, we all go. Isn't that right, lads?

Under the cover of an early-morning mist we make it back to our trenches, Charlie carrying the Captain on his back the whole way until the stretcher bearers came for him. As they lifted him up, Captain Wilkie held Charlie by the hand:

(CAPTAIN WILKIE.) Take my watch, Peaceful. You've given me more time on this earth.

(CHARLIE. *Admiring the watch.*) It's wonderful, sir. Ruddy wonderful.

FRONT LINE

The next time they send us up the line it is into the Wipers' salient itself, where our own lines had encroached into the enemy territory. Everyone knew Fritz had us surrounded and overlooked on three sides – they could chuck all they wanted into our trenches and all we could do was grin and bear it. We had a new company commander, Lieutenant Buckland. He told us how things were:

(LIEUTENANT BUCKLAND.) If we give way then Wipers will be lost. Wipers must not be lost.

He didn't say why it mustn't be lost but he was doing his best. He was straight out from England, very properly spoken, but he knew even less about fighting this war than we did. He seemed younger than any of us, even me.

WIPERS

As we march through Wipers I wonder why it is worth fighting for at all. There was no town left; nothing you could call a town anyway. Rubble and ruin, more dogs and cats than civilians. None of us sang. None of us talked.

TRENCHES

When we get to the new trenches, there is a sickly-sweet stench about the place that has to be more than stagnant mud and water. We all knew well enough what it was, but we don't speak about it.

I'm on stand-to the next morning.

The mist rises over no-man's-land.

I see in front of me a blasted wasteland.

No fields or trees,

not a blade of grass –

simply a land of mud and craters.

I see unnatural humps

scattered over there beyond our wire:

the unburied,

some in field-grey uniforms and some in khaki.

There's a German soldier lying in the wire

with his arm stretched heavenwards,

his hand pointing.

There are birds up there,

and they are singing.

We're back down in the dug-out after stand-to, brewing up when the bombardment starts.

   (*Sound: bombardment.*)

It doesn't stop for two whole days. They are the longest two days of my life. We can not talk. We can not think. When I do manage to sleep I see the hand pointing skywards, and it is Father's hand, and I wake shaking. I cry like a baby and not even Charlie can comfort me. We want it to stop, even though we know that when it's over they'll be coming for us with the gas maybe, or the flame-thrower, or the grenades, or the bayonets. Let them come. I just want this to stop. I want it to be over.

When at last it does stop we are ordered out on to the firestep, bayonets fixed, eyes straining through the smoke that drifts across in front of us.

(*Sound: music – Holst's 'Mars' from* The Planets.)

Then out of the smoke we see them come, their bayonets glinting, one or two at first, but then hundreds, thousands.

The firing starts all along the line – and I'm firing too, not aiming, just firing. Firing. Firing. Loading my rifle and firing. And still the Germans do not stop. They come towards us, an invincible army. I can see their wild eyes as they reach our wire. It's the wire that stops them, and those that find the gaps are shot down before they ever reach our trenches. The others have turned now and are stumbling back. I feel a surge of triumph welling inside me, not because we have won, but because I have stood with the others. I have not run.

(TOOTHLESS OLD LADY.) Y'ain't a coward, are you?

No, old woman, I am not.

Then the cry goes up:

'Gas! Gas! Gas!'

(*Sound: bell.*)

It is echoed all along the line. For a moment we are frozen in terror. We see it rolling towards us, this dreaded killer cloud we have heard so much about. Its deadly tendrils are searching ahead, feeling their way forward in long yellow wisps, scenting me, searching for me. Then seeing me, the gas turns and drifts straight for me:

(TOMMO.) Christ! Christ!

I tell myself I will not breathe. I see men running, staggering, falling. I have to breathe now. I can't run without breathing. Half-blinded by the gas mask I trip and fall. My gas mask has come off. I pull it back on, but I have breathed in and already my eyes are stinging, my lungs are burning. I am coughing, retching, choking. I don't care where I'm running so long as it's away from the gas – and then I'm out of it.

(*TOMMO wrenches off his mask, gasping for good air.*)

I look up through blurred and weeping eyes. A Hun in his own gas mask is standing over me, his rifle pointing at my head.

(*TOMMO braces himself.*)

(GERMAN SOLDIER.) Go boy! Go, Tommy, go!

So by the whim of some kind and unknown Fritz I survive and escape.

FIELD HOSPITAL

Later, at the field hospital, I hear that we counter-attacked, retaking our front-line trenches; but, from what I could see all around me, it was at a terrible cost. All that attack and all that death, for nothing. No gains on either side. I line up with the rest of the walking wounded to see the doctor. He washes out my eyes, examines them, and listens to my chest.

(DOCTOR.) You were lucky. You can only have caught a whiff of it.

As I walk away I pass the others who have not been so lucky, rows of them, lying stretched out in the sun, many of them faces I knew, and would never see again: corpses.

ESTAMINET

That evening I was in the estaminet drowning my anger in beer. And it was anger I was drowning, not sorrows. In my befuddled state I even thought of deserting: I'd make my way to the English Channel and find a boat. I'd get home somehow.

I look around me. There must have been a hundred or more soldiers in the place that evening but they all looked as alone as I felt. It's stiflingly hot in there and the air is thick with cigarette smoke – like the gas. I can hardly breathe. It gives me the shakes. I went outside to get some air.

(ANNA.) Tommy?

It was her. She was carrying out a crate of wine bottles.

(ANNA.) You are ill?

We stood for some moments. I want to speak, but I don't trust myself. I felt suddenly overwhelmed by tears, by a longing for home and for Molly.

(ANNA.) How old?

(TOMMO.) Sixteen.

(ANNA.) Like me. I have seen you before I think?

(*TOMMO nods.*)

(ANNA.) My name is Anna.

(TOMMO.) My name is Tommo.

(ANNA.) It's true then, every English soldier is called Tommy.

(TOMMO.) No, not Tommy; I'm Tommo.

STABLE

I told her I worked on a farm and she took me into the stable and showed me her father's carthorse. He was massive and magnificent. Our hands met as we patted him. She kissed me then, brushed my cheek with her lips.

ROAD

I left her and walked back to camp under the high-riding moon, singing at the top of my voice:

(TOMMO. *Singing.*) Oranges and Lemons say the bells of St Clement's…

CAMP

Charlie greeted me at the camp with a smirk:

(CHARLIE.) You won't be so ruddy happy, Tommo, not when you hear what I've got to tell you. Our new sergeant. It's only Horrible-Bleeding-Hanley.

6

BARN

Nearly four o'clock.

There is the beginning of day in the sky, not the pale light of dawn yet, but night is certainly losing its darkness.

CAMP

We get plenty of letters at rest camp – they come far swifter to the front than they do at home. Charlie has been fretting about Molly and has written to her every day. Then one morning, we both receive a letter in Molly's handwriting. Charlie opens his – and weeps. I open mine –

(MOLLY.) My dear Tommo,

I write to say that I have had a darling boy. Charlie and I agreed on his name before you both went away: Tommo, after his brave uncle. One day, when this dreadful war is over, we shall be together again and young Tommo will see his father and his uncle for the first time and smile. Big Joe already smiles at him. And little Tommo has Big Joe's great grin – and Charlie's (black) hair, and your (hazel) eyes. Because of all this I love him more than I can say.

Your Molly.

I caught sight of Charlie. He was wiping away his tears. He was looking more determined than ever – and I could see why.

(CHARLIE.) Sergeant Hanley, what a nice surprise. I heard you'd joined us.

(SERGEANT HANLEY.) I'm warning you, Peaceful, I've got my eye on you. One step out of line...

(CHARLIE.) Don't worry about me, Sergeant. I'll be as good as gold. Cross my heart and hope to die.

ROAD

Once again we find ourselves marching up into the trenches, along with hundreds of others, 'to stiffen the line' they told us, which could only mean one thing: a big attack was expected and we would be in for a packet of trouble.

(*Sound: shell whine.*)

TRENCH

The blast throws us all to the ground, it is the first shell of thousands. Our big guns answer almost at once, and the world above us erupts.

(*Sound: bombardment.*)

Every heavy gun the Germans have seems to be aimed at our sector. It's terrifying. I find myself curled into a ball on the ground and screaming for it to stop. Then I feel Charlie lying beside me, folding himself around me to protect me.

(CHARLIE. *Singing.*) Oranges and Lemons say the bells of St Clement's...

– and soon I am singing with him, singing instead of screaming. 'You owe me five farthings...' (*Etc.*) And before we know it the whole dug-out is singing along with us. But the barrage goes on and on and on, until in the end neither Charlie nor 'Oranges and Lemons' can drive away the terror that is engulfing me, invading me, destroying any last glimmer of courage I have left. All I have now is my fear.

When the German attack comes, it falters before it ever reaches our wire. When they turn and run, we wait for the whistle and then go out over the top.

(*Sound: whistle.*)

NO-MAN'S-LAND

I go because the others go, moving forward as if in a trance, as if outside myself altogether. *(Sound: boom!)* There is blood pouring down my face, and my head is burning, such a terrible pain, and I feel myself falling, and it's warm and comforting and so quiet…

7

BARN

Twenty-five to six.

Twenty-five minutes to go. How shall I live them? Should I eat a hearty breakfast? I don't want it. Shall I scream and shout? What would be the point? Shall I pray? Why? What for? Who to?

No. They will do what they will do. General Haig has signed and he is God out here. Haig has confirmed the sentence. He has confirmed that 'Private Peaceful will die, will be shot for cowardice in the face of the enemy at six o'clock on the morning of the 25th of June 1916.'

They say there's soon going to be an almighty push all the way to Berlin. I've heard that before. They say the regiment is marching up the road towards the Somme. It is late June, summer here and at home, the Somme here for our troops, and…

The firing squad will be having their breakfast by now, sipping their tea.

No one has told me exactly where it will happen. I don't want it to be in some dark yard with grey walls all around. I want it to be where there is sky and clouds and trees, and birds.

(*Sound: muffled ordinance.*)

CONCRETE DUG-OUT

I wake to the muffled sound of machine-gun fire, to the distant blast of the shells. The earth quivers and trembles about me. It must be night and I am lying wounded somewhere in no-man's-land, looking up into the black of the sky. But then I try to move my head a little and the blackness begins to crumble and fall in on me, filling my mouth, my eyes, my ears. It is not the sky I am looking at, but earth. I am buried, buried alive – they must have thought I was dead and buried me. But I am not dead. I'm not! My fingers scrabble, clawing frantically at the earth – and then I feel something. Another body. And I hear a voice:

(CHARLIE.) Thought we'd lost you, Tommo. The same shell that buried you killed half a dozen of the others. You were lucky. Your head looks a bit of a mess, though. Me, I can't feel my legs. I think I've lost a lot of blood.

(TOMMO.) Where are we, Charlie?

(CHARLIE.) Middle of bloody no-man's-land, that's where, some old German dug-out.

(TOMMO.) We'd best stay put for a while, hadn't we, Charlie?

(SERGEANT HANLEY.) Stay put? Stay put? You're worse than your brother, Peaceful. Our orders are to press home the attack and then hold our ground. Only fifty yards or so to the German trenches. On your feet, all of you.

(*No one moves.*)

(SERGEANT HANLEY.) What in hell's name is the matter with you lot? On your feet, damn you! On your feet!

Then I hear myself speaking, quietly at first:

(TOMMO.) I think we're all thinking the same thing, Sergeant. You take us out there now and the German machine-guns will mow us down. Maybe we should stay here and then go back later when it gets dark? No point in going out there and getting ourselves killed for nothing, is there Sergeant?

(SERGEANT HANLEY.) Are you disobeying my order, Private Peaceful?

(TOMMO.) No, I'm just letting you know what I think. What we all think.

(SERGEANT HANLEY.) And I'm telling you, Peaceful, that if you don't come with us when we go, it won't be field punishment like your brother got, it'll be a court martial. It'll be the firing squad. Do you hear me, Peaceful? Do you hear me?

(TOMMO.) Yes, Sergeant. I hear you. But the thing is, Sergeant, even if I wanted to, I can't go with you because I'd have to leave Charlie behind, and I can't do that. He's wounded. I don't think he can walk, let alone run. I'm not leaving him.

(SERGEANT HANLEY.) You miserable little worm, Peaceful. I should shoot you right where you are and save the firing squad the trouble. The rest of you, on your feet. I want you men out there. It's a court martial for anyone who stays.

One by one the men get unwillingly to their feet, each one preparing himself in his own way, a last smoke on a shielded cigarette, a silent prayer.

(SERGEANT HANLEY. *Screaming.*) Let's go! Let's go!

   (*Sound: the German machine-guns open fire.*)

(TOMMO.) Poor beggars.

Then Charlie speaks:

(CHARLIE.) I'm not sure I'm going to make it, Tommo. I want you to have this.

(*CHARLIE takes off his watch.*)

(CHARLIE.) It's a wonderful watch, this. It will never let you down. If you wind it regular, time will never stop and when you get back home, little Tommo can have it. He's got all the time in the world.

Then Charlie spoke no more. And I must have slept, because when I open my eyes, there is Sergeant Hanley staring at me from under his helmet, cold hate in his eyes.

We waited, but by nightfall there was no sign of the others who had joined the Sergeant on that futile charge.

NO-MAN'S-LAND

In the dark of the night, we stumble back to our trench across no-man's-land, me carrying Charlie, giving him a piggyback all the way.

BARN

It wasn't a proper trial. They'd made up their minds I was guilty before they even sat down. I had three of them: a brigadier and two captains. I told them everything. I wasn't going to hide anything:

(TOMMO.) Yes, I did disobey Sergeant Hanley's order. The order was stupid, suicidal – we all knew it was – and I had to stay behind to look after my brother, Charlie.

They knew a dozen or more got wiped out in that attack. They knew I was right, but it made no difference. Because there's a big push coming, they want to make an example of someone.

The brigadier said I was a worthless man. Worthless.

Molly didn't think I was worthless. Charlie didn't think so either. Nor Mother, Big Joe, Father.

The whole court martial took less than an hour. That's all they gave me. One hour for a man's life.

Sound: a distant church bell chimes six o'clock.

TOMMO slowly leaves the stage.

Sound: a volley of shots.

Sound: music.

The End.

TORO! TORO!

Stumbling upon a bull in Spain

As I was wandering in the hills of Andalucía in the south of Spain in the autumn of 2000, I came, quite by chance, upon a farm where they breed black bulls for the *corrida*, the bullring. The very same day I found myself on a wooded hillside looking down at the ruined village of Sauceda.

This remote village had been bombed and burned out in the early stages of the Spanish Civil War – the first time in Europe that deliberate aerial bombardment of a civilian population had ever happened. Since then, in Guernica, Warsaw, London, Dresden, Hiroshima and thousands of other cities, towns and villages all over the world, this practice has sadly become all too commonplace.

My first glimpse of that herd of magnificent black bulls, and then the sighting of Sauceda in ruins, served to inspire me to sit down and write *Toro! Toro!*. But I had some research to do first, into bullfighting, and into the Spanish Civil War. This terrible war, fought in the 1930s, was a struggle between the socialist left, the Republicans, and the fascist right, the Nationalists, for the control of Spain. After many years of vicious fighting, the Nationalists, under their fascist leader General Franco, won. Only on Franco's death, in 1975, did Spain become a democracy.

So here's *Toro! Toro!* a story of children who lived through that war, a story of Spain, of bulls and bullfighting.

Michael Morpurgo

Toro! Toro! is to be performed by one actor who speaks as ANTONITO and as all the characters denoted in (BRACKETS.). He also dances as the bull in the bullring, and as PACO, the Black Phantom, *El Fantasmo Negro*. Where appropriate, occasional English can be spoken as Spanish. The scenes should flow seamlessly, the action dramatised boldy, the music and the music of the words performed majestically.

Toro! Toro! was first performed at the Salberg Studio, Salisbury Playhouse, 19 April 2010:

ANTONITO	Gary Turner

Director & Designer	Philip Wilson
Lighting Designer	Peter Hunter
Sound Designer	Alex Twiselton
Movement Director	Isabel Sheppard
Deputy Stage Manager	Eleanor Randall
Guitar & Music Director	Pete Aves
Trumpet	Chris Holmes

Thanks to Philip Wilson, Xavier Mascarell, Fred Stableford, Otto and Hazel Reade and Michael Morpurgo.

Toro! Toro!

A bare circle of a stage which suggests the arena of la corrida, *a bullring, set against a backdrop of the Spanish hills and a broad, blood-red sky.*

Martial, funereal music plays solemnly, which segues into a sung Catholic Mass.

A 45-year-old man, ANTONITO, enters, crosses himself with habitual respect, and carefully lays out a matador's costume, el traje de luces, *a suit of lights, as if he was dressing a corpse: shimmering embroidered jacket, the tight three-quarter-length breeches, the black hat, the crimson cape attached to the* muleta *stick.*

The sounds of the modern street are heard.

ANTONITO: Franco is dead. November 20th, 1975, and Europe's last Fascist dictator has died. My country of Spain is unsure what to do. Flags are fluttering, apologetically, at half-mast. On his deathbed, Franco, The Generalissimo, said a kind of sorry:

(FRANCO.) I ask pardon of all my enemies – as I pardon with all my heart those who declared themselves my enemy – although I did not consider them to be so.

ANTONITO: Well, I beg your pardon, Francisco Franco Bahamonde, but if we weren't your enemy, then why…?

(*He wipes away an angry tear.*)

… But I'll begin at the beginning shall I?

(*The sounds of an old farmyard: horses, cattle, chickens, dogs, pigs, goats etc.*)

I was born in a small farmhouse just outside the village of Sauceda on *el uno de Mayo* – the 1st of May, 1930. Mayday. There was my older sister, Maria – nine years older than me to the day – and Mother, and Father. Just the four of us. We had uncles and aunts and cousins all around, of course

– the whole village was like one big family. But we can skip all that. It was another birth about five years after my own that really began it all.

The farm didn't belong to Father. Hardly anyone owned the land they worked – we just farmed it. It was hard, but I knew little of that. For me it was a magical place to grow up. There were cork forests all around: we'd harvest the cork, cutting it off the trees every nine years – to make corks for wine bottles, of course! For *Jerez*, for sherry.

We had our little black pigs wandering everywhere too; and dozens of goats for our milk and cheese; and chickens – we were never short of eggs for a *tortilla*. And we had mules, for bringing the cork down from the hillsides. But mostly it was cows we kept. Not those reddy-brown *Rositos* you often see out in the countryside. No, ours were black: black and beautiful and brave. My father reared only black bulls. We must have had fifty or sixty of them, counting all the calves. They were magnificent –

(FATHER.) The best in all Andalucía!

ANTONITO: – my father said. As a small boy I'd spend hours standing on the fence, just watching them, marvelling at their wild eyes, their wicked-looking horns, their shining coats.

(*As he describes the bulls, he subtly takes on their characteristics.*)

They lifted their heads and snorted at me; they pawed the ground, kicking up great clouds of dust and dirt. They were the noblest, the most exciting creatures on God's earth.

(*He struts and stamps and snorts like a magnificent bull. Music.*)

At that age I had no real idea why we kept them. They were just out there, grazing in their *corrals*, part of the landscape of my life – and life seems simple enough when you're five years old! Then, *he* came – and nothing was ever to be simple again.

(*Sound: thunderclap.*)

There was a terrible thunderstorm the night he came. Father teased me:

(FATHER.) Are you frightened?!

(ANTONITO.) No!

ANTONITO: – which wasn't true. Maria laughed:

(MARIA.) Yes you are!

(ANTONITO.) I'm not!

ANTONITO: And I went outside into the storm with Father to prove it.

(*Sound: the thunder continues to rumble.*)

I followed Father's swinging lantern across the yard, hoping and praying the lightning wouldn't see the lantern and strike us dead!

The mother cow was lying down in the barn – and two little white feet were already showing from under her tail! Father crouched down behind her, took hold of the feet, and tried to pull. There was some grunting and groaning – from Father as well as the cow – and then...a calf slipped out into the world! And there it lay, shining black and steaming in the straw, shaking its head free of the clinging membrane.

(FATHER.) *Toro.* We've got a fine little bull.

ANTONITO: Father knelt over him, lifted his head and poked a piece of straw down his nostrils.

(FATHER.) It will help him breathe better.

ANTONITO: The mother was trying to get to her feet – Father moved smartly away, grabbing me to him. She was bellowing at us – she didn't want us anywhere near her calf. But try as she might, she couldn't get up. She just didn't have the strength.

(FATHER.) That calf has to drink, and soon, or he won't live. And he won't be able to drink unless she stands up.

ANTONITO: So I joined in:

(ANTONITO.) Get up! Get up! *Levánta-te!*

(*He jumps up and down.*)

ANTONITO: But she didn't. She couldn't. She was completely exhausted by her efforts.

(FATHER.) Only one thing for it.

ANTONITO: Crouching down beside her, Father stripped some milk from her udder into a bucket. Then he poured it into a bottle with a teat on it, lifted the calf's head, and dribbled the milk down his throat until at last he suckled.

(FATHER.) We've got a brave one here. I'll hold him, Antonito. You feed him.

ANTONITO: And he handed me the bottle.

(ANTONITO.) There you go. Good boy. You're a beauty you are. You're going to be the finest bull in all of Spain!

ANTONITO: He sucked and sucked and sucked, and as he sucked, his eyes looked into mine...

...and mine looked into his...

...and I loved him.

(ANTONITO.) Let's call him Paco.

(FATHER.) That's a fine name. And he's a brave bull!

ANTONITO: I could see Father was becoming more and more anxious about Paco's mother. And it was only a couple of hours before she breathed one last sigh... In that same night I witnessed my first birth. And my first death.

Paco was soon up and on his feet. I crouched in the corner, and watched his first staggering steps. Every few hours after that I would go to the barn to feed him. I wasn't tall enough and I had to get on to an upturned bucket, otherwise he couldn't suck from the bottle properly. I'd stand up there, wave the bottle at him and call him over to me.

(ANTONITO, *whistling encouragement*.) Paco! Hey, Paco!

ANTONITO: He'd suck so strongly that it was all I could do to hold on to the bottle.

To begin with, Maria would always be there with me.

(MARIA.) It looks easy. Let me have a go.

ANTONITO: Paco went wild and butted her up the bum! … Maria never asked to feed him again.

Those days playing mother to Paco were the happiest of my life. Paco followed me everywhere. I'd tie a rope round his neck and take him for walks up into the cork forests. He just seemed to follow along naturally. He kept nudging me to remind me he was there, or to remind me it was feeding time – again. The two of us were inseparable. Then one breakfast, Mother smiled at me, sadly:

(MOTHER.) You've done a fine job, Antonito. Your father's very proud of you, and so am I. No one could have given Paco a better start in life, no one. But if he's to make a proper bull, then you mustn't handle him any more. No one must. We'd be gentling him too much. He's got to grow up wild. It's what he was born for.

ANTONITO: I had no idea what she was talking about. But I could tell that they were going to take Paco away from me. I began to argue – but Mother interrupted:

(MOTHER.) And besides, he'll be better off with a cow for a mother. There's one that's just lost her own calf. She'll have the milk to spare.

(ANTONITO.) But she'll know Paco's not her calf. She won't feed him!

ANTONITO: Father chewed on his bread. Mother looked at Father. Father looked at me:

(FATHER.) We'll flay her dead calf and dress Paco in the fresh hide. She'll take to him soon enough.

(ANTONITO.) But Father!

(FATHER.) From now on, Antonito, you keep away from Paco, you understand? Or else he'll be of no use to anyone. Keep away!

ANTONITO: I cried and cried and cried – and for two days refused all food. I hated Father and Mother and I made up my mind that I would never speak to them ever again. Maria saw how I felt. So she slipped me outside to see Paco in the *corral.*

(MARIA.) Look at him. Doesn't he look happy?

ANTONITO: He was frisking about with his nurse mother in his borrowed skin.

(MARIA.) If he's happy, then you should be happy, Antonito. That is what you want, isn't it?

(*He nods.*)

ANTONITO: I guessed it wasn't the end of the world after all. And I decided that I *could* see Paco if I wanted to – but in secret! I'd wait until the coast was clear, then steal out to his *corral.* Maria could keep watch and I'd stand on the fence and call him over.

(*He whistles.*)

I thought he might have forgotten me – but he soon came trotting over – and licked my hand! I think he must have liked the salty taste of it. It didn't seem to matter to him that no milk came out. Then his nurse mother came wandering over and shook her horns at me, but I kept on my side of the fence and she soon lost interest.

Maria worried that we'd be discovered, and kept urging me to come away. But luckily, Father and Mother never did find out about our secret meetings – not then; not ever.

Paco grew fast in his first year. He grew horns, and he played at fighting with the other yearlings, mock battles which he always won.

(*He acts this out.*)

He was sleek and fast. Sometimes I would help Father move the herd to fresh pastures. Even then, when the bulls were running together, you could pick out Paco easily. He was the finest and noblest bull-calf in the herd. He would be at the front with the big bulls, the five-year-olds – nearly as old as me.

I never spoke of him to anyone but Maria. She warned me over and over again not to become too fond of him.

(MARIA.) All animals have to die, Antonito.

ANTONITO: But I was six years old, and death meant nothing to me. I never gave it a second thought. It only happened to old people, old animals. Paco was young. I was young.

I was walking back home from school one day when I saw some bigger boys hanging about by the well in the village. A couple of them were playing at something in the street, egged on by the others. It was a game I hadn't seen before, so I stopped to watch.

One of the boys, my cousin Morelo, was pushing a strange-looking contraption. It had a single wheel and two handles, like a wheelbarrow, but with horns sticking out at the front: bull's horns. I'd seen pictures in the village café of matadors with the big capes, of bulls charging them. I'd always thought of it as some kind of dance. Cousin Morelo was running at cousin José with the bull machine, and, at the last moment, José sidestepped neatly, so that the horns passed him by and charged only into his swirling crimson cape. Each time everyone cried:

(BOYS.) *Olé! Olé!*

(*He performs the manoeuvre, balletic.*)

ANTONITO: I was entranced. Then José had a stick in his hand, and the chant went up:

(BOYS) Stick-it-in! Stick-it-in! Stick-him-with-the-*banderilla*!

ANTONITO: They were all jeering and laughing and clapping, it was nasty – I turned and ran all the way home, tears pouring down my cheeks. I found Maria collecting eggs.

(ANTONITO.) It's a dancing game isn't it? Tell me it's just a dance.

ANTONITO: She kissed away my tears.

(MARIA.) It's all right, Antonito. Like you say, it's a game, just a dancing game.

(ANTONITO.) And will Paco have to play it?

(MARIA.) Animals don't think like we do, Antonito. Animals are animals, people are people.

(ANTONITO.) What do you mean?

(MARIA.) Don't be silly, Antonito.

(ANTONITO.) You're the silly one, not me – you're a silly cow!

ANTONITO: Maria mooed at me and charged me, and I charged her back. In the scuffle we broke a lot of eggs... Mother was furious.

But the next day we had news that *Tío* Juan, Uncle Juan was coming to stay and the smashed eggs were quickly forgotten.

Juan was the most famous person in our whole family. I could only remember having actually seen him just once before at a christening: tall and strong. Wherever he was, people crowded around him – *El Bailarin*, they called him:

The Dancer. He was a matador, a real bull-dancer. He lived in Malaga, miles and miles away over the hills. I'd never been there, but I knew it was a big and important town, and that my Uncle Juan had danced with the best bulls in Spain in the bullring there, and in Ronda too.

He arrived late the next evening.

(*Sound: cicadas.*)

We put up the long table outside, and gathered chairs and stools and benches wherever we could find them, and then everyone came. There must have been twenty of the family there, cousins – Morelo and all – all feasting on our giant *paella* – the slowly cooked rice, delicious with onion, *conejo*, chicken…

(*A traditional Andalucían food song.*)

I couldn't take my eyes off Uncle Juan, though he never once smiled at me all through dinner, even when I caught his eye – his eyes seemed to look right through me. The talk was all of the *corrida* in Algar the next day.

(JUAN.) It will be crowded – you'll have to be there early to find a place.

ANTONITO: Suddenly Uncle Juan put his hand on my shoulder:

(JUAN.) And Antonito will come too. It will be his first *corrida*. He is old enough now. He may be little, but he's a little man, *mi pacito* – my little man!

ANTONITO: And everyone clapped and I laughed, and I loved it. Juan smiled. And his eyes twinkled in the gathering darkness. The wind sighed through the high pine trees and the sweet song of the cicadas filled the air.

Everyone spoke earnestly now, their faces glowing in the light of the lanterns. And the talk was of war, a war I had not even heard of until that night.

They spoke in hushed voices, leaning forward, as if out in the night there might be enemy ears listening, enemy eyes watching. All I understood was that some hated *Generalissimo* from the north, was sending soldiers from the Spanish Foreign Legion into Andalucía in the south, to attack us, and that our soldiers – Republicans they called them – were gathering in the hills to fight them.

The argument was simple enough even for a six-year-old to understand. To fight or not to fight. To resist or not to resist. They talked in raised whispers. Father wasn't sure:

(FATHER.) If we go about our lives as usual, they're bound to leave us alone.

ANTONITO: Then Uncle Juan finally spoke, and everyone fell silent:

(JUAN.) It is all about freedom. A man without freedom is a man without honour, without dignity, without nobility. If they come, I will fight for the right of the poor people of Andalucía to have enough food in their bellies, and I will fight for our right to think as we wish and say what we please.

ANTONITO: It was very late. I was getting cold. So I crept back into the house and upstairs. As I was passing the room we had prepared for Uncle Juan, I noticed that the door was open. A moth was flitting around the lamp, its shadow dancing on the ceiling. All Juan's clothes were spread out on the bed – his matador's costume, *el traje de luces*, a wonderful suit of lights, glittering with thousands of embroidered beads; and beside it his shining black hat, and his crimson cape. The costume was very heavy, but I managed to shrug it on. It swamped me, and the huge hat rested on the bridge of my nose. Now the *muleta*, the crimson cape. I whirled it, I swirled it, I floated it and I flapped it, and all the while I danced in front of the mirror.

(ANTONITO. *Dancing as he has described.*) *Olé! Olé!*

ANTONITO: Someone began clapping behind me – I daren't turn around.

(JUAN.) You dance well, Antonito. No bull would catch you, not in a million years!

ANTONITO: Uncle Juan was grinning in the mirror.

(ANTONITO.) I have a bull of my own. He's called Paco, and he's the noblest bull in Spain.

(JUAN.) Your father has told me of him. One day I may dance with him in the ring in Ronda.

ANTONITO: He took the black hat off me, and the beautiful costume, and the cape. I caught sight of myself in the mirror. I was an ordinary six-year-old again, not a matador any more, just Antonito.

(JUAN.) You want to help me practice?

ANTONITO: He stood up straight and tall, nearly touching the ceiling, and stamped his feet, flapping the crimson cape:

(JUAN.) *Toro! Toro!*

ANTONITO: And I charged. Again and again I charged, and each time I was swathed in his great cape and had to fight my way out of it.

(*He performs this.*)

(JUAN.) We dance well *mi torocito*, my little bull. But now we must both be off to bed. I have some serious dancing to do tomorrow. Wish me luck. Pray for me.

ANTONITO: I woke up early next morning, and we set off, riding in the cart. The road was full of horses and mules and other carts all going to Algar for the *corrida*.

La Corrida.

The bullring was a cauldron of noise and heat, the whole place pulsating with excitement.

(*First Trumpet.*)

As the trumpet sounded, Uncle Juan strode out into the ring, magnificent in his embroidered costume. There were other men behind him, *banderilleros* and *picadors.* When I asked Maria what they did, she didn't seem to want to tell me. Instead, she took my hand, held on to it tight and would not let go.

All around the ring the crowd was on its feet and applauding wildly. Uncle Juan stopped right in front of us and lifted his hat to us. I felt so happy.

(*Second Trumpet.*)

A second trumpet – and there was the bull trotting purposefully out into the centre of the ring, a glistening giant of a creature, black and beautiful in the sun. Then he saw Uncle Juan and the dance began.

(*The Dance of the Toreador. Third Trumpet. The crowd roars. JUAN dances with the bull.*)

Then came the third trumpet and the mounted *picadors* ride in, their horses padded up, and the bull charges – the first *banderilla* goes in, deep into the bull's shoulder, and he charges again, and again, and there's blood down his side, a lot of blood, and the crowd is baying for more, he feels the pain, but he knows no fear: he's a brave and noble bull. The *banderillos* tease him, maddening him, decorating his shoulders with their coloured darts, leaving him standing there defiant, his tongue hanging in his exhaustion, in his agony.

(*Another Trumpet. Then Silence.*)

(*Whispers.*) Uncle Juan steps forward and takes off his hat. He stands before the bull, his crimson cape outstretched.

(JUAN.) *Toro! Toro!*

ANTONITO: And the bull charges him – once, twice, three times, and each time Uncle Juan draws the bull's horns harmlessly into the cape, a dance of precision, the *faena* of *El Bailarin*. It seems now that the bull no longer has the strength to do anything but stand and pant and wait. I see the silver sword held high in Juan's hand, produced like a magician from under his crimson cape. I see it flash in the sun – and then I see no more because I bury myself in Maria's shoulder –

(ANTONITO.) Take me out! Take me out!

ANTONITO: We struggle our way through the crowd and I catch a last glimpse of the bull – his carcass dragged away by the mules, limp and bleeding. And Uncle Juan is strutting about the ring, soaking up the applause, catching the thrown flowers.

(*ANTONITO is sick.*)

(ANTONITO.) It's what will happen to Paco, isn't it?

(MARIA. *Wiping his face.*) Yes. But Paco doesn't know it. It will be just a few minutes at the end of his life. It's all over so quickly.

(ANTONITO.) Never! I won't let it happen to him, Maria, I won't! I'm going to run away with him and I'll never come back!

ANTONITO: I meant what I said. But there were other distractions, and as time went by…well…

The war was no longer just talk around a family *paella*. Just a few weeks after the bullfight in Algar, the first soldiers came to the village: our soldiers, Republican soldiers. Some were wounded – on crutches, or with their heads bandaged, sitting in the café. There was talk of others hiding in the houses in the village or up in the cork forests. Mother explained:

(MOTHER.) The war is not going well for them – for us. We have to feed the soldiers. It will give them the strength to fight again.

ANTONITO: Almost daily now Mother would send Maria and me into the village with eggs and bread, *jamón*, cheese for the soldiers. We delivered it to the café, and sometimes they'd be singing and smoking and drinking. I knew they were our soldiers, but they looked rough all the same and I was frightened of their eyes, even when they smiled at me.

At home, Father was troubled:

(FATHER.) Fighting an invader – I can understand that. But Spaniard against Spaniard, cousin against cousin? Civil war? It is *un*-civil. It is wrong, wrong.

Mother interrupted:

(MOTHER.) But they are defending us, defending freedom, and we must help them.

ANTONITO: In all this time, I began to think again about Paco and how he might escape. I lay awake at night, thinking it over. My idea wasn't clever, but it was simple. I knew that to separate Paco from the herd, to release him on his own, would be impossible; even if I succeeded, sooner or later he would nose out the others and come running back to them. So, I would have to release them all, all of them together, and drive them as far as I could up into the cork forests where they could lose themselves and never be found. Even if a few were caught, Paco might be lucky. At least he stood some chance of freedom, some chance of avoiding the horrors of the *corrida*.

I lay in bed, forcing myself to stay awake. I waited until the house fell silent about me. The sound of Father's deep snoring was enough to convince me that it was safe to move. I was already dressed under my blankets, and I had a rope. I stole out of the house and across the moonlit yard. The dogs whined at me, but I patted them, soothed them, and they didn't bark. I headed down the farm track, out of sight of the house, and then out over the fields.

The cattle shifted as I came closer. They were nervous, unsettled by this strange night-time visitor. I opened the gate of their *corral*. They stood looking at me, snorting, still, shaking their horns a little.

(ANTONITO. *Whistling softly*.) Paco! Paco! It's me. It's Antonito!

ANTONITO: He walked slowly towards me, his ears twitching and listening all the time as I sweetened him closer. Then, as he reached the open gate, the others began to follow, shuffling through the open gateway. Then they were trotting – then jostling…then galloping, charging past me, stampeding.

Sound: the galloping herd of bulls.

I was knocked senseless – and when I awoke Paco stood over me, looking down at me. All the other cattle were gone.

I got slowly to my feet. I was a little bruised, my cheek was cut – I could feel the blood, sticky under my hand when I touched it – but I was not badly hurt at all. Paco stared at me. I had the rope, but I didn't need it. We would go as far as we could, as fast as we could, before dawn. Where? I had no idea. As we climbed the tracks up into the hills, I felt a surge of triumph. Paco was free, and now I would keep him free! I didn't stop to think what it would mean to Father to lose his precious herd of cattle – all that mattered was that Paco would not suffer that terrible death in the bullring. I had done it!

We climbed on, higher and higher into the early morning mist, until the last of the night was gone and a hazy white sun rose over the hills. We came suddenly into a clearing. On the far side was a stone hut, in ruins, and beside it a small, circular, stone *corral*. There were several like this scattered through the cork forests, built for gathering cattle or sheep or goats. Paco followed me in and I shut the sturdy gate behind us. He nuzzled the grass. I lay down in the shelter of the wall, and fell asleep.

The warming sun woke me – that or the cry of vultures. They were circling above us in the blue. The mist had all gone. Paco lay beside me, licking his nose. I lay there for a while, listening to the breeze and to Paco chewing the cud.

(*Sound: drone.*)

I heard the sound of distant droning, like bees, like thousands of bees. I thought I must be imagining things, but then Paco was on his feet and snorting. The vultures were suddenly gone. The droning was coming closer, closer, until it became a throbbing, angry roar that filled the air.

(*The throbbing roar is thunderous.*)

Then I saw them, flying low over the ridge towards us, dozens of them – airplanes with black crosses on their wings. They came right over us.

(*He curls up in terror, covering his ears.*)

Paco was going wild, circling the *corral,* frantic, looking for a way out. The planes passed overhead and, when I thought it was safe, I climbed up onto the wall. That's when they started diving, their engines screaming, diving on Sauceda, onto the village, diving on my home.

(*Sound: distant crunch of the air raid.*)

I saw the smoke of the bombs – and then I heard the crunch of the distant explosions. Father and Mother and Maria were down there, somewhere in all that smoke and fire. And then the planes were gone. And it was silent. I went out of the gate and closed it firmly behind me.

(ANTONITO.) I'll be back, Paco. I'll be back, I promise.

ANTONITO: The last I saw of him he was looking over the gate, tossing his head, pawing at the ground – and then I was gone, down into the woods and out of his sight. I could hear him calling me, his bellowing echoing all around the hills. Below me the smoke drifted along the valley, as if a new mist had come down, and I ran faster and faster towards home.

(*A blood-red light – the fierce crackle of fire.*)

I stood in the yard and watched my home burn, the flames licking out of the windows. I could hear anger in those flames, the roaring, crackling, spitting. I did not call out for Father or Mother or Maria. No one could survive that inferno.

How long I stood there I don't know. I saw the dogs. They were lying dead, all of them, near the water trough. The flames died down – they had nothing more to burn. Only the walls of our farmhouse remained, charred and smouldering.

Then I cried, cried out:

(ANTONITO.) Mama! Papa! Maria!

ANTONITO: I called for them, called for them, until my throat was raw. I knew it was hopeless to go on, but I called and called some more.

Then I hear voices. Soldiers. Hundreds of them, moving up the valley towards the farm, towards the village – not our soldiers, but other soldiers in different uniforms. I dart inside the barn, looking for somewhere to hide, anywhere. The voices, the enemy soldiers are coming closer. I scramble up the rickety ladder into the hayloft, burrow myself deep into the hay, and lie still. I could hear them outside in the yard now, laughing. I hated them, but I gritted my teeth to stop myself from crying out. I heard heavy footsteps in the barn below me:

(SOLDIER 1.) Let's burn this barn down.

(SOLDIER 2.) No, Later. *Vámanos.*

ANTONITO: As the soldiers went, I lay absolutely still, silent, and only when I was sure it was safe, I crept out from under the hay, down the ladder and out into the yard.

The whole farm was deserted again. I hared across the yard, ducked under the fence and sprinted across the field towards the hills and safety.

When I looked down into the valley below, I saw the smoking ruins of Sauceda beyond our farm. And then the shooting began.

(*Random, prolonged rifle fire, faint screams. Then silence.*)

That was when the survivors of the bombing – all my Uncles and Aunts, all my cousins, Morelo, José, all the good people of Sauceda – that was when they all were massacred.

(*He hides his head in his hands.*)

The sound of that shooting still echoes in my head all these years later. I had no mother, no father, no sister, no family, no friends, no home, no village. All gone from me in one day.

But I still had Paco.

It was dusk before I reached the clearing and the stone *corral* again. I called for Paco as I approached the gate –

(*He whistles.*)

– but he did not come. He did not come because he was not there. There was a gaping hole in the stone wall: Paco had burst his way through and was gone.

Exhausted, I lay down to sleep. When I closed my eyes I saw Mother's face, and Father's, and Maria's, and our home on fire. I heard the shooting and the crackling of flames. When I awoke, I was relieved it was morning. I was hungry. It gnawed at my stomach. I *had* to find food. I chewed on acorns – better than nothing. I drank water from the streams – when you're hungry, even water seems to fill you up – for a while, at least. I slept on the forest floor, under the canopy of the trees, wherever I could find shelter. I always kept to where the forest was thick and would hide me.

I don't know how many days – or weeks – I wandered the hills. My head swam, I was overcome by weakness, by drowsiness. Then one day I fell and just could not get up again. I lay there looking up at the waving branches, at the shifting clouds. I heard the wind sighing through the forest and remembered, long long ago it seemed, a lantern-lit dinner outside the farmhouse, the time when Uncle Juan came, the day before the bullfight. I remembered his words:

(*Sound: subliminal cicadas.*)

(JUAN.) A man without freedom is a man without honour, without dignity, without nobility…

ANTONITO: I could hear his voice speaking to me. I could see his face. I must be dreaming. He is smiling as he did in the *corrida*, lifting me up as he'd done when I'd danced the bull-dance with him at home. Now I can feel him carrying me. He is talking to me:

(JUAN.) You'll be all right, Antonito. You'll be all right. I'll look after you now.

ANTONITO: I reached out and touched his face…

* * *

I am lying in a cave. I can smell smoke –

(*He momentarily panics.*)

– cooking. I can hear people talking, men and women and children.

(WOMAN.) It's Juan's little nephew, from Sauceda. Poor little thing. He's dying, you know.

ANTONITO: And I cried out inside:

(ANTONITO.) No, I'm not! I am *not* dying. I won't let myself die. I want to see Paco again. I want to find him.

ANTONITO: And so my fever died down, and I started to eat, and very slowly I regained my strength.

There might have been fifty people living up in the cave. Perhaps half were freedom fighters, like Uncle Juan. The rest were refugees, hiding out in the hills, terrified to return home for fear of the soldiers, or the police, the *Guardia Civil.* Food was scarce; we had only what was brought up to us at night from the villages, or gathered from the forest around.

I didn't have to tell Juan about the bombing of Sauceda. He knew about it. Everyone knew about it. I was the only survivor, and only I knew why that was. If I hadn't chosen that night to set Paco free, then I would have been dead in the ruins of the farmhouse, or shot down trying to escape.

The more I thought of it, the less I felt I had a right to have survived, to be alive. I was there because I'd been committing a dreadful crime, releasing all Father's bulls into the wild, his whole pride and joy, robbing him of his lifetime's work. When I cried now, it wasn't from hunger or grief – but from shame.

Uncle Juan held me tight:

(JUAN. *Wiping ANTONITO's tears away with his thumbs.*) They were terrible things you saw, Antonito. So cry, cry all you want. But when you've done crying, then be brave again, be my brave little bull, *mi torocito.* Evil, Antonito, must be fought, not cried over. You understand me?

(*He smiles at ANTONITO and laughs.*)

We are few, but we are strong. Even the beasts are on our side, do you know that? Have you heard about *El Fantasmo Negro de Maracha*, The Black Phantom of Maracha?

(ANTONITO.) *El Fantasmo Negro*? The Black Phantom?

(JUAN.) This is not just one of my tales, Antonito, this is true. There are patrols out in the hills – soldiers, the *Guardia Civil* looking for us. Don't worry, Antonito, they won't catch us. We ambush them; we fight them; we send them running like rabbits. But when they sent out a patrol from Maracha – maybe twenty of them, from the *Guardia Civil* – they thought they saw something move in amongst the trees. They started shooting – and out of the trees he comes: the Black Phantom! You know what he is, *El Fantasmo Negro*?

(*ANTONITO scarcely believes what he's hearing.*)

A *nobile*, a young fighting bull. He came charging at them. And what did they do? They dropped their rifles and ran! But one of them who didn't run fast enough, got himself tossed in the air. When the others turned to look, the bull had vanished, like a phantom. It was as if he had never been there. And yet there were hoof prints, the hoof prints of a young bull.

ANTONITO: Paco! It had to be Paco! Paco was alive! He was out there, somewhere. He was looking for me!

I had so much to say, so much I was longing to tell Uncle Juan, but I couldn't say anything without confessing to what I'd done. So all I said was:

(ANTONITO.) That bull: he must be the bravest bull in the whole world.

(JUAN.) You're right, Antonito. And if he can be brave, then so can you.

ANTONITO: The story of the Black Phantom lifted our spirits. There was the sound of laughter again; and when the children got together to act out the drama, I got up and joined in. I was the *nobile*, the young bull. I was Paco.

(*He paws the ground, tosses his head, and then charges.*)

They all screamed and ran away – just like rabbits, just like the patrol in the forest at Maracha.

(*Shooting echoes about the hills – the game instantly stops – then silence.*)

(JUAN.) We have to move deeper into the hills. The *Guardia Civil* are getting nearer every day.

ANTONITO: So began our long march. We only had a pair of mules, and they were needed to carry what few blankets, what little food we had, as well as the youngest children. The food soon ran out.

(*Sound: rain – ANTONITO looks up into the sky, blinking back the rainfall.*)

And then the rains came, turning the tracks into streams, into quagmires. We could only go as fast as the slowest amongst us – two old ladies, twin sisters, from Algar.

(JUAN.) You both should ride instead of the children.

(TWIN SISTER.) No, Juan. It is the young that must live. And besides, we have our sticks.

ANTONITO: One morning, after yet another cold night in the open air, we were getting ready for yet another day's march when I noticed that the two old ladies hadn't moved. They were lying together under a tree, hugging each other for warmth, their sticks lying by their side. They lay so still, so absolutely still, one with her forefinger on her lips as if willing the world to hush.

We buried them where they lay. Juan never smiled again after that. His great heart seemed to have broken. But we all needed him, willed him to bring us through somehow. He was the one person who gave us hope. He led us on, deeper into the hills, and from the top of every pass we saw even more hills, higher hills lost in the clouds. And still the rain poured down. And on we trudged. And as we went, others joined us, more freedom fighters, more refugees, till our fifty became two hundred.

One dawn, as we came out of the woods into a narrow valley with a cheerful river running through it, the rain stopped and the sudden sun warmed our backs. And we sang.

(*He sings an Andalucían folk song with a Republican flavour.*)

Ahead of us, we saw a cluster of farmhouses in a clearing, apparently deserted. But as we sang, from out of the houses they appeared, one by one at first, then in twos and threes, in their dozens, fearful, bedraggled, pale. As they recognised that we were like them, their faces lit up, and they came running. We were greeted like conquering heroes. Stranger hugged stranger. We wept out of sheer joy that we were together, that we were alive.

I made my way through the crowd of people, down to the river for a drink. There was an older girl there, a young woman, really, standing in front of me, gaping at me, wide-eyed.

(MARIA.) Antonito!

(ANTONITO.) Maria?

ANTONITO: We clung to each other, clung on for dear life.

(ANTONITO.) And Mother? Father?

(*She shakes her head.*)

(MARIA.) When you couldn't be found, I was sent out to look for you, and then the planes came, and the farm was bombed, and I ran back, and the house was on fire and I couldn't get near it. I looked for you everywhere, called for you, and the pigs and the goats and the chickens were running everywhere in a wild panic, and all the time the planes were screaming, screaming down on the farm and bombing. All I could think of was getting away, so I ran and ran, and I wandered the woods for days – before meeting a charcoal burner, who fed me and brought me here to hide up in the hills with all the others. We've been here for weeks and weeks. There's very little food to go round and we're all terrified that the soldiers might come.

(ANTONITO.) You won't have to worry any more. Uncle Juan is here with his soldiers, and they'll look after us.

(MARIA.) What were you up to when the planes came? I looked everywhere.

ANTONITO: Should I lie? Should I tell the truth?

But just then, Uncle Juan came to us.

(JUAN.) I've decided. You take a mule and you both go tonight, you go now.

(ANTONITO.) Why?

(JUAN.) Because we are too many here. There's not enough food to go round. Because sooner or later we'll be discovered and we'll have to fight. We will fight, and fight as well as we can. But we are few and they are many. I don't want you to be here when it happens.

(MARIA.) No, Uncle Juan, we're staying with you –

(JUAN.) No arguments, Maria. It's the only way. I want you to go to Malaga, to my mother's house – kiss her for me, Antonito. Look after her. Be a son to her. Will you do this for me?

(ANTONITO.) Yes.

(JUAN.) Follow the river down into the valley. You'll join the road there. The *Guardia Civil* won't harm you. You are children. They have children of their own.

ANTONITO: He led us to where the mule stood, white in the moonlight. He held us for a moment, kissed us both on the forehead, then lifted each of us up onto the mule.

(JUAN.) *Vaya con Dios.* Go with God.

ANTONITO: We kept turning in the saddle to see him, until the darkness took him from us and we were alone.

We did see soldiers, lots of them, but they ignored us. Several times the *Guardia Civil* stopped and questioned us. Maria told them truthfully:

(MARIA.) We are visiting our Great Aunt in Malaga.

ANTONITO: And each time they nodded us through. Wherever we stopped for the night people fed us and gave us shelter. If I learned one thing on that last long journey, it is that men and women have as much kindness in them as they do evil, more kindness, much more.

When at last, after many days' travel, we reached Malaga and Juan's house, I did just what he'd told me. I kissed his mother and, in time, I made myself a son to her. Together, Maria and I looked after her. I think she knew all along that her real son, Juan, would not be coming home.

We never did discover what happened to him. Like so many thousands of others in the Civil War, he just disappeared, *desaparecido.* Gone, but he's not forgotten.

In my new school, in Malaga, the children spoke with awe about *El Fantasmo Negro.* There were stories of how he'd been seen wandering the streets at night in Cortes; or spotted by a shepherd in the hills outside Jerez; even in the castle at Gaucin. He had surprised a column of soldiers, one hundred strong; and chased a *Guardia Civil* officer through the streets of El Colmenar. I knew the stories couldn't be all true – though I hoped they were. But the tales of *El Fantasmo Negro* kept hope alive even when the war was lost. I hoped that I might see Paco again one day; but as time passed it became only the faintest of hopes, based on a story I only half believed.

Quite a few years later – I was nineteen, nearly twenty by now – I had a job cutting cork in the forests near Maracha. I was on my own, and tired after a long day's work. I make myself a small fire, and after supper I lie down beside it.

The mules hobble nearby. I fall asleep easily, and I dream. I dream that Paco is lying there beside me, chewing the cud, licking his nose. He is so close I can smell his milky breath.

(*Sound: bull noises.*)

I wake up suddenly –

(*He looks around expectantly – but is disappointed.*)

Paco isn't there. Of course he isn't. It was a dream.

I get to my feet – and then I notice the grass nearby – it has been flattened. I feel it. It's warm. Then I see the hoof marks, the hoof marks of a massive bull. Paco had found me.

(*A faint whistle echoes.*)

For years after that, whenever I worked in the cork forests, I always looked out for Paco, even though I knew it was quite impossible he could still be alive. But it didn't matter. I was a happy man.

(*The sounds of the present, November 1975, return.*)

And today I am a happy man… Sad too. Not sad that an old man has died. Not sad for Franco, but sad that it's taken this long for me to apologise, to face up to the truth – that I ran away with Paco, and let my mother and father and family and friends and my village die: the tiny village of Sauceda, destroyed by the world's first deliberate air attack on civilians, a bombardment that soon bred the destruction of Guernica, and then of Warsaw, of London, of Dresden, Hiroshima, and all the air-raids on ordinary people in all the wars ever since.

But I am happy, because there is hope. Today there are no clouds: the sun shines down on us from our vast Spanish skies. And as long as we're truthful, and honest, and brave – as brave as a bull – there will be a future.

He struts the bull-dance one last time.

Toro! Toro! – Toro! – Toro!

The lights brighten – a trumpet of the fiesta blasts – as the stage fades to black.

The End.

THE MOZART QUESTION

The Violinist

It is difficult for us to imagine how dreadful was the suffering that went on in the Nazi concentration camps during the Second World War. The enormity of the crime that the Nazis committed is just too overwhelming for us to comprehend. In their attempt to wipe out an entire race they caused the death of six million people, most of them Jews. It is when you hear the stories of the individuals who lived through it – Anne Frank, Primo Levi – that you can begin to understand the horror just a little better, and to understand the evil that caused it.

For me, the most haunting image does not come from literature or film, but from music. I learned some time ago that in many of the camps the Nazis selected Jewish prisoners and forced them to play in orchestras; for the musicians it was simply a way to survive. In order to calm the new arrivals at the camps they were made to serenade them as they were lined up and marched off, many to the gas chambers. Often they played Mozart.

I wondered how it must have been for a musician who played in such hellish circumstances, who adored Mozart as I do – what thoughts came when playing Mozart later in life. This was the genesis of my story, this and the sight of a small boy in a square by the Accademia Bridge in Venice, sitting one night, in his pyjamas on his tricycle, listening to a busker. He sat totally enthralled by the music that seemed to him, and to me, to be heavenly.

Michael Morpurgo

The Mozart Question was first performed at Bristol Old Vic's Studio on 7 February 2007 with the following company:

PAOLO   Andrew Bridgmont

Director   Julia McShane
Lighting Designer   Susan Dean

Scamp Theatre subsequently toured the production to the Edinburgh Fringe Festival, the New End Theatre, Hampstead, and across the UK with lighting design by Sally Ferguson.

It was subsequently performed in Sweden, in translation, under the title *Aldrig Mozart (Never Mozart)*, presented by Teater Fredag, directed by Anders Alnemark, where Paolo has also been played by an actress, Paola.

With thanks to Alison Reid, Jennifer Sutherland and Louise Callow, and Michael Morpurgo.

Characters

PAOLO

is a violinist approaching his 50th birthday.

He plays the characters in his story, indicated (THUS.)

Ideally the actor is an accomplished violinist. His violin can also be used as an abstract object in the course of the play.

The Mozart Question

Unaccompanied Vivaldi violin is played live. Lights up to reveal
PAOLO LEVI: neat, trim, cardigan, corduroy trousers – shabbily elegant
– comfortable slippers. He is playing at an open window through which
the Venetian light bounces off the water. A chair or two. Music on a
music stand. A violin case. A small table with a tea pot and a fine mug
and a fresh mint plant. An electric kettle.

He finishes the music.

Silence.

PAOLO: I like to practice by the window. I can watch the world
go by on the canal. And I love to be near water, to look out
on it. I love the light that water makes.

(*He turns.*)

Paolo Levi. Almost 50. In a fortnight it's my birthday
concert.

(*Pause.*)

You'll know who I am, of course. I played my first major
concert when I was 13 – I've played every major concert
hall the world over, in front of Kings and Queens –
Presidents. I'm best known for Vivaldi but I'm equally
at home with jazz, or Scottish fiddle music, or Bach. And
yes my English is good, even though I was born here
in Venice. Language is like music: you learn it through
listening. But I'm talking too much. I talk too much when
I'm nervous. When I go to the dentist's I talk. Before a
concert I talk.

(*He puts the kettle on. Plucks peppermint tea leaves. When the kettle*
has boiled he pours.

Silence.)

I like to keep this room empty. Sound needs space to
breathe – just the same as we need air. I like silence.
There should be silence after a performance. It's part of
the music. There shouldn't be applause. I don't like to
be interrupted. Applaud the music, the composer, but
certainly not the musician.

(*PAOLO sits on the chair by the window, rests the violin on his drawn-up knees, plucks the strings to tune it.*)

I have a confession to make. I have a secret. And someone
once told me that all secrets are lies. The time has come, I
think, not to lie any more.

(*Pause.*)

I will tell you a story.

(*Pause.*)

I will start with my father.

(*The rhythmic sound of meticulously snipped barber's scissors.*)

Papa was a barber. He kept a little barber's shop just
behind the Accademia, near the bridge, just two minutes
from here. We lived above the shop, Mama, Papa and me
– but I spent most of my time downstairs, in the barber's
shop, sitting on the chairs and swinging my legs, smiling
at him and his customers in the mirror, sweeping up the
hair clippings for a few lira my father would tip me, just
watching him. I loved those days. I loved him. I must have
been about nine years old.

(*He speaks as if he was living it again, seeing it again.*)

Papa was infinitely deft with his fingers, his scissors playing
a constantly changing tune. It seemed to me like a new
improvisation for every customer. He would work always
in complete silence, conducting the music of his scissors
with his comb. His customers knew better than to interrupt
the performance. Some would close their eyes as Papa

worked his magic; others would look back in the mirror at me and wink.

(*The sound of shaving lather being whipped up and applied, the swish and slap of the razor on the strap, the rasp of the blade removing stubble.*)

Shaving was just as fascinating to me, just as rhythmical too: the swift sweep and dab of the brush, the swish and slap of the razor as Papa sharpened it on a strap, then each time the miraculous unmasking as he stroked the foam away to reveal a recognisable face once more.

After it was all over, he and his customers did talk, and all the banter amongst them was about football – or sometimes the machinations of politicians – and women. They laughed a lot, and then the next customer would take his seat and a new silence would descend before the performance started and the music of the scissors began again.

Papa wasn't just the best barber in all of Venice – everyone said that – he was a musician too, a violinist. But strangely he was a violinist who never played the violin. I never heard him play, not once. I only knew he was a violinist because Mama told me so. She had tears in her eyes whenever she told me about it. That surprised me because she was not a crying woman.

(MAMA. *Tears in her eyes.*) He was so brilliant as a violinist, the best in the whole orchestra.

(YOUNG PAOLO.) Why doesn't he play any more, Mama?

(MAMA. *Turning away.*) You will have to ask him that yourself, Paolo.

PAOLO: So I did.

(YOUNG PAOLO.) Papa, Papa! Why don't you play the violin any more?

(PAPA. *With a shrug.*) People change, Paolo. Times change.

PAOLO: Papa was never a great talker at the best of times, but I could tell he was hiding something. I kept on at him. Every time he refused to talk about it I became more suspicious, more sure he had something to hide.

One morning, while my father was snipping away in the barber shop below, my mother relented:

(MAMA.) If I show you the violin will you promise me you'll not ask Papa again?

(YOUNG PAOLO.) What violin?

(MAMA.) Promise?

(YOUNG PAOLO.) Promise.

(MAMA.) And you're never ever to tell Papa I showed you. He'd be very angry. Promise me now.

(YOUNG PAOLO.) I promise. I promise faithfully.

PAOLO: I stood in my parents' bedroom and watched as Mama climbed up on a chair to get the violin down from where it had been hidden on top of the wardrobe. It was wrapped up in an old grey blanket. I knelt on the bed beside her as she pulled away the blanket and opened the violin case. It smelt musty. The lining inside was faded and worn to tatters. Mama picked up the violin with infinite care, reverential. Then she handed it to me.

I stroked the polished grain of the wood, which was the colour of honey – dark honey on the front, and golden honey underneath. I ran my fingers along the black pegs, the mottled bridge, the carved scroll. It was so light to hold, I wondered at its fragile beauty. I knew at once that all the music in the world was hidden away inside this violin, yearning to come out. I longed to be the one to let it come out, to rest it under my chin, to play the strings, to try the bow. I wanted there and then to bring it to life, to have it sing for me, to hear all the music we could make together. So I asked my Mama:

(YOUNG PAOLO.) Can I play it?

(MAMA. *Taking fright.*) Papa might hear downstairs. He'd be furious with me for showing you.

(YOUNG PAOLO.) Why, Mama?

(MAMA.) He never wants it to be played again. He hasn't so much as looked at it in years.

(YOUNG PAOLO.) But why?

(MAMA.) You promised if I showed you you'd not ask any more questions. You now know it exists, Paolo. But you never saw it, understand? And from now on I don't want to hear another word about it, all right?

(YOUNG PAOLO.) But Mama!

(MAMA.) You promised me, Paolo.

PAOLO: She laid it back safely in its case, wrapped it in the blanket, and put it back on top of the wardrobe.

And that was that.

Then late one summer's evening I was lying half awake in my bed –

(*The distant sound of an unaccompanied violin – Bach, Vivaldi.*)

– when I heard the sound of a violin. I thought Papa must have changed his mind and was playing again at last. But then I heard him and Mama talking in the kitchen below, and realised that the music was coming from much further away.

I listened at the window. Over the sound of people talking and walking, over the throbbing engines of the passing water buses, came the sweet sound of the violin from somewhere beyond the bridge. In my pyjamas I stole past the kitchen door, down the stairs and out into the street. It was a warm night, and quite dark. I ran up over the bridge and there, all on his own, standing by the wall in the square, was an old man playing the violin, his violin case open at his feet.

No one else was there. No one had stopped to listen. He was so engrossed in his playing that he didn't notice me at first. I could see now that he was much older even than Papa. Then he saw me.

(*The playing stops.*)

(BENJAMIN.) Hello. You're out late. What's your name?

(YOUNG PAOLO.) Paolo. Paolo Levi. My Papa plays the violin. He played in an orchestra once.

(BENJAMIN.) So did I, all my life. But now I am what I always wanted to be, a soloist. I shall play you some Mozart. Do you like Mozart?

(YOUNG PAOLO.) I don't know. I know the name, but I don't think I've ever listened to any of his music.

(BENJAMIN.) He wrote this piece when he was even younger than you – I would guess that you're about seven?

(YOUNG PAOLO. *Affronted.*) I'm nine.

(BENJAMIN.) Well, I'm sixty-two – and Mozart wrote this when he was just six years old. He wrote it for the piano, but I can play it on the violin.

(*Mozart.*)

PAOLO: As he played, others came and gathered round for a while before dropping a coin or two in his violin case and moving on. I didn't move on. I stayed. The music he played to me that night touched my soul. It was the night that changed my life for ever.

Whenever I crossed the Accademia Bridge after that I always listened out for him. I never told Mama or Papa. I think it was the first secret I kept from them. But I didn't feel guilty about it, not one bit. After all, hadn't they kept a secret from me? Then one evening, the old man let me hold his violin, showed me how to hold it properly, how to draw the bow across the strings, how to make it sing. The moment I did that, I knew I had to be a violinist.

Signor Horowitz, as he told me he was called, became my first teacher. Every time I ran over the bridge to see him he would show me a little more, how to tighten the bow just right, how to use the resin, how to hold the violin under my chin using no hands at all and what each string was called.

(YOUNG PAOLO.) Papa has a violin at home but he doesn't play it any more. He couldn't anyway, because it's a bit broken. I think it needs mending. Two of the strings are missing, the A and the E, I think, and there's hardly a hair left on the bow at all. But I could practice on it if it was mended, couldn't I, Signor Horowitz?

(*Pause.*)

(BENJAMIN.) Bring it to my house sometime and leave it with me. I'll see what I can do.

PAOLO: It wasn't difficult to escape from home unnoticed. I just waited till after school. Mama was still at the laundry round the corner where she worked. Papa was downstairs with his customers. To reach the violin on top of the wardrobe I had to balance a suitcase on the chair and then climb up. It wasn't easy but I managed. I ran through the streets hugging it to me.

Signor Horowitz lived along a winding passage, up a narrow flight of stairs in one small bare room where his music could breathe. On the walls were lots of posters:

(BENJAMIN.) Some of the concerts I have played in, Paolo: Milan, London, New York. Wonderful places, wonderful people, wonderful music. It is a wonderful world out there. There are times when it can be hard to go on believing that. But always believe it, Paolo, because it's true. And music helps to make it so. Now, show me that violin of yours.

(*BENJAMIN studies it closely, holding it up to the light.*)

(BENJAMIN.) A very fine instrument. It's a bit on the large side for a young lad like you… But a big violin is better than no violin at all. You'll grow into it.

(YOUNG PAOLO.) And when it's mended, will you teach me? I've got lots of money saved up from my sweepings.

(BENJAMIN.) Sweepings?

(YOUNG PAOLO.) In Papa's barber shop.

(BENJAMIN.) I'll teach you for nothing! You're my best listener. You're my lucky mascot. When you're not there, everyone walks by and my violin case stays empty. Then you come along and sit there and they stop to listen and leave their money. A lesson or two will just be paying you back, Paolo. I'll have the violin ready as soon as I can and then we can start your lessons.

PAOLO: It was a fortnight before the violin was mended. I dreaded what Mama or Papa might do if they discovered it was missing. But they didn't, and my lessons began.

(*Music: violin practice.*)

I took to the violin as if it had been a limb I had been missing all my life. And it sang with the voice of an angel.

(*Music.*)

(BENJAMIN.) I think this instrument was invented just for you, Paolo. Or maybe you were made for it. Either way it is a perfect match.

PAOLO: We would finish every lesson with a cup of mint tea made with fresh mint. I loved it.

My secret was safe, I thought. But secrets are never safe, however well hidden. Sooner or later truth will out.

One day with the lesson over, we were drinking tea when Benjamin looked across at me:

(BENJAMIN. *Serious.*) It is strange, Paolo, but I feel I have known you before, a long, long time ago. Your name: Levi. It's a common enough name, I know – but his name was Levi too. It is him you remind me of. I am sure of it. He was the youngest player in our orchestra, no more than a boy really. Gino, he was called.

(YOUNG PAOLO.) But my father is called Gino! Maybe it was him? Maybe you played with my father? Maybe you know him?

(BENJAMIN.) It can't be possible. *(Staring at YOUNG PAOLO.)* No, it can't be. The Gino Levi I knew must be… I have not heard of him in a long while. But you never know, I suppose. Maybe I should meet your papa, and your mama too. It's about time anyway. You've been coming for lessons for a good while now. They need to know they have a wonderful violinist for a son.

(YOUNG PAOLO.) No, you can't! He'd find out! You can't tell him. You mustn't! It's a secret. Mama showed me Papa's violin and made me promise never to say anything, never to tell Papa, and I've kept it a secret all this while, from Mama too, mending the violin, the lessons, everything…

(BENJAMIN.) Secrets, Paolo, are lies by another name. You do not lie to those you love. A son should not hide things from his mama or papa. You must tell them your secret, Paolo. If you want to go on playing the violin, you will have to tell them. If you want me to go on teaching you, you will have to tell them. And now is usually a good time to do what must be done, particularly when you don't want to do it.

(YOUNG PAOLO.) Will you come with me? I can only do it if you come with me.

PAOLO: So, Signor Horowitz carried Papa's violin, and held my hand all the way back home. I was dreading having to make my confession. I knew how hurt Mama and Papa would be. All the way I rehearsed what I was going to say over and over again. Mama and Papa were upstairs when we came in:

(YOUNG PAOLO. *Blurting it all out.*) Mama, Papa: this is Signor Horowitz, he is my violin teacher. I didn't really steal Papa's violin, I just borrowed it to get it mended, and to practice on –

PAOLO: I was terrified – but they didn't look angry. In fact, they weren't looking at me at all. They were just staring at Signor Horowitz, unable to speak. He spoke for them:

(BENJAMIN.) Your mama and papa and me, I think perhaps we do know one another. We played together once, did we not? Don't you remember me, Gino?

PAOLO: Papa looked at him.

(PAPA.) Benjamin?

(BENJAMIN. *To MAMA.*) And if I'm not mistaken, Signora, you must be little Laura Adler – all of us violins, all of us there, and all of us still here. It is like a miracle. It *is* a miracle.

(*Traditional Jewish string music.*)

PAOLO: Suddenly it was as if I wasn't in the room at all – the three of them seemed to fill it, arms around each other, and crying openly, crying through their laughter. I stood there mystified, trying to piece together what I'd just heard, all that was going on before my eyes. Mama played the violin too! She had never told me that!

(BENJAMIN.) You see, Paolo, didn't I tell you it was a wonderful world? Twenty years! It's been twenty years or more since I last saw your mama and papa. I had no idea they were still alive. I always hoped they survived, hoped they were together, these two little lovebirds, but I never really believed it, not really.

PAOLO: Mama was drying her eyes. Papa was so overcome, he couldn't speak. They all sat down then, hands joined around the table, unwilling to let each other go, afraid this reunion might turn out to be no more than a dream. Signor Horowitz – Benjamin was the first to recover:

(BENJAMIN.) Paolo was about to tell you both something, I think. Weren't you, Paolo?

(YOUNG PAOLO.) Well…yes… Signor Benjamin has been my violin teacher – he is the best teacher in the world! But please don't be angry. Don't be cross…

PAOLO: But Papa and Mama were glowing with joy:

(MAMA.) Didn't I say Paolo would tell us, Gino? You see, Paolo, I often take down my violin, just to touch it, to look at it. Papa doesn't like me to, but I do it all the same, because this violin is my oldest friend. Papa forgives me, because he knows I love this violin, that it is a part of me. When it went missing, I knew it had to be you. Then it came back, mended miraculously. And then, after school, you've started to be late home; and when you haven't been home, the violin has always been gone too. I told Papa, I told him you'd tell us when you were ready. We put two and two together; we thought you might be practicing somewhere, but it never occurred to us that you were having lessons, that you had a teacher – and certainly not that your teacher was Benjamin Horowitz, who taught us and looked after us like a father all those years ago.

(YOUNG PAOLO.) But you told me it was Papa's violin, that he'd put it away and never wanted to play it again? And what do you mean Signor Benjamin was your teacher too?

PAOLO: The three of them looked at one another. I knew then they all shared the same secret, and without a word passing between them they were deciding whether they should reveal it, if this was the right moment to tell me. Papa invited me to the table to join them:

(PAPA.) Mama and me, we try never to speak of this, because the memories we have are like nightmares, and we want to forget. But you told us your secret. There is a time for truth, it seems, and it has come. Truth for truth.

(*Throughout the revelation of the secret a sound and music score plays under the speaking.*)

(PAPA.) The three of us were brought by train to the concentration camp from all over Europe: Benjamin from Paris, Mama from Warsaw, and me from here, from Venice. We were all musicians, all Jewish. We survived only because we were able to say 'yes' to one question put to us by an SS officer on arrival at the camp:

(SS OFFICER.) Is there anyone amongst you who can play an orchestral instrument, who is a professional musician?

(PAPA.) I didn't know that when I stepped forward I would immediately be separated from my family...

Playing was very hard because our fingers were so cold that sometimes we could hardly feel them and we were weak with hunger. Sickness had to be hidden. The SS were always watching. In those rehearsals the three of us met. Benjamin was a good deal older than me and your mama. We were very much the babies of the orchestra, we were barely twenty. Why the orchestra was rehearsing, who we would be playing for, we did not know and we did not ask. We played Mozart, a lot of Mozart.

A medley of Eine kleine Nachtmusik*, minuets etc. And Johann Strauss Viennese waltzes.*

(PAPA.) The repertoire was for the most part light and happy – *Eine kleine Nachtmusik*, minuets, dances, marches. And Johann Strauss was popular too, waltzes, waltzes, always waltzes.

At first we gave concerts only for the SS officers. You just had to pretend they were not there. You simply lost yourself in the music – it was the only way. Even when they applauded you did not look up. You never looked them in the eye. You played with total commitment. Every performance was your best performance, not to please them, but to show them what you could do, to prove to them how good you were despite all they were doing to humiliate you, to destroy you in body and soul. We fought back with our music. It was our only weapon.

PAOLO: Then Benjamin interrupted:

(BENJAMIN.) You see, Paolo, your papa could speak no Polish, your mama knew no Italian, but their eyes met when they were playing. They shared a joy in music-making, and they fell in love – the whole orchestra knew it, before they did! 'Our little lovebirds', we called them. For everyone else in the orchestra they represented hope, the future.

PAOLO: But Mama wasn't so sure:

(MAMA.) I don't know about that, Benjamin. Our love numbed the pain, protected us from the fear we were living through, from the horror going on all around. But we all shared a shame. We were being fed while others were not.

(*Pause.*)

PAOLO: Papa continued:

(PAPA.) One cold morning with snow on the ground, we were made to assemble out in the compound with our instruments and ordered to sit down and play.

(*Mozart plays over trains screeching, wagons unloading, barked orders etc.*)

(PAPA.) A train arrived, the wagons packed with new prisoners. Once they were all out they were lined up and then divided. The old and young and frail were herded past us as we played, on their way – so they were told – to the shower blocks. The able-bodied, those fit for work, were taken off towards the huts. And all the while your mama and Benjamin and I and the orchestra, we played our Mozart. We all understood what our Mozart was for: it was to calm each new train-load of frightened souls, to give them a false sense of security. We were part of the deadly sham. We all knew of course that the shower block was a gas chamber.

Week after week we played, month after month, train after train. And twenty-four hours a day the chimneys of the crematorium spewed out their fire and their smoke and their stench. Until there were no more trains; until the day the camps were liberated.

We were all emaciated by now. It was unlikely that any of us would survive. Your Mama and I walked out of the camp. That was the last time we saw Benjamin. Until now.

PAOLO: Papa stopped talking. Mama leaned towards me:

(MAMA.) We walked across a shattered Europe, playing our violins for bread and shelter. We were still playing to survive. And we came here to Venice, to your papa's home. And he smashed his violin. But I kept mine. It was my talisman, my saviour and my friend. I wouldn't destroy it, sell it, abandon it. It had brought me through all the horrors of the camp, brought us safely across Europe, back to Papa's home in Venice. It had saved our lives.

Papa has never played a note of music again – he can hardly bear to hear it, which is why I haven't played my violin in all these years. I've kept it on top of the wardrobe, hoping against hope that Papa might change his mind and be able to love music again.

In time we were blessed with a child, a boy we called Paolo – a happy ending. And now, Paolo, you have brought Benjamin and your papa and me together again. So another happy ending.

PAOLO: And I asked:

(YOUNG PAOLO.) What happened to you, Benjamin? How did you come to be in Venice?

(BENJAMIN.) I found my way back to Paris after a while. I played again in my old orchestra. I married a French girl, Françoise, a cellist who died only recently. So I came to Venice because Vivaldi was born here – I have always loved Vivaldi above all other composers. I play in the streets – not just for the money, but because I could not bear not to play the violin. Music kept me alive in the camp, and music has been my constant companion ever since. I couldn't imagine living a single day of my life without it. Which is why I would dearly like to go on teaching Paolo if you both would allow it.

PAOLO: Benjamin looked at Papa. Papa looked at me. I looked at Mama:

(MAMA.) Can we hear Paolo play, Gino? Can we hear him, please?

(*Pause.*)

(PAPA.) So long as it's not Mozart.

Vivaldi's 'Winter' movement from the Four Seasons *on unaccompanied violin.*

PAOLO: Benjamin turned to Papa:

(BENJAMIN.) He has a great and wonderful talent, your son, a rare gift you have both given him.

PAOLO: And then my father said, quietly:

(PAPA.) Then it must not be wasted.

PAOLO: So every day without fail I went for my violin lessons with Benjamin in his little apartment. Papa could not bring himself to listen to me playing, but sometimes Mama came along with me and listened, and afterwards she always hugged me so tight it hurt. I began to play in the streets alongside Benjamin, and whenever I did the crowds became bigger and bigger.

(*Bach 'Double Violin Concerto' unaccompanied.*)

One day amongst those watching and listening was Papa. He walked me home afterwards, saying nothing until we were outside our front door:

(PAPA.) So, Paolo, you prefer playing the violin to sweeping up in my barber's shop, do you?

(YOUNG PAOLO.) Yes, Papa. I'm afraid I do.

(PAPA.) Well then, I can see I shall just have to do my sweeping up myself. I shall tell you something, Paolo, and I want you never to forget it. When you play I can listen to music again. You have made music joyful for me once more, and that is a wonderful gift you have given me. You go and be the great violinist you should be. I shall help you all I can. You will play heavenly music and people will love you. Mama and I shall come to all your concerts. But you have to promise me one thing: that until the day I die you will never play Mozart in public. Never Mozart. Promise me.

PAOLO: So I promised. I have kept my promise to Papa all these years. He died two weeks ago, the last of the three of them to go. At my fiftieth birthday concert I shall be playing Mozart, and I shall be playing it on Mama's violin, and I shall play it so well that he will love it, they all will love it, wherever they are.

(*Silence.*

Mozart violin music – which then builds into the whole orchestral version – and we hear church bells, the chuntering of boats, talking and laughing and music, music from the streets. PAOLO stops playing. The music continues.)

Music belongs in the streets, where Benjamin played it, where I played it with him, not in the concert halls.

(*Pause.*)

It was time to tell the truth. Because secrets are lies…

Mozart violin soars.

The End.

OTHER ADAPTATIONS BY SIMON READE

Pride and Prejudice
Jane Austen
9781840029512

The Scarecrow and His Servant
Philip Pullman
9781840028997

Not the End of the World
Geraldine McCaughrean
9781840027365

Private Peaceful & Other Plays
(Private Peaceful / Aladdin and the Enchanted Lamp /
The Owl Who Was Afraid of the Dark)
Michael Morpurgo, Philip Pullman, Jill Tomlinson
9781840026603

Twist Of Gold
Michael Morpurgo
9781849432061

Private Peaceful
(Single Edition Playtext)
Michael Morpurgo
9781849435017

OTHER TITLES BY SIMON READE

Dear Mr Shakespeare:
Letters to a Jobbing Playwright
9781840028294

WWW.OBERONBOOKS.COM

Follow us on www.twitter.com/@oberonbooks
& www.facebook.com/oberonbook